# THE
# GROWTH
# SPIRAL

# THE
# GROWTH
# SPIRAL

*The Proven Step-by-Step
Method for Calculating
and Predicting Growth
Potential in Your Church*

# ANDY ANDERSON

BROADMAN
& HOLMAN
PUBLISHERS

Nashville, Tennessee

© Copyright 1993 ● Broadman Press
All rights reserved
4230-13
ISBN: 0-8054-3013-x
Dewey Decimal Classification: 268
Subject Heading: Sunday Schools—Growth
Library of Congress Catalog Card Number: 92-44805
Printed in the United States of America

Unless otherwise indicated, all Scripture references are from the *King James Version* of the Bible. All Scripture references marked NKJV are from the *New King James Version*. Copyright © 1979, 1980, 1982, Thomas Nelson, Inc., Publishers.

Note: Growth Spiral software is available from Church Information System (CIS) of the BSSB to assist a church when working Growth Spirals. The software is available for IBM or IBM compatible computers using the MS-DOS operating system. The software is designed to provide Growth Spiral information about classes, departments, or entire Sunday Schools and print in either spiral or table format. For more information or to order the Growth Spiral software, call CIS at 1-800-325-7749.

**Library of Congress Cataloging-in-Publication Data**

Anderson, Andy, 1927-
 The growth spiral / by E.S. (Andy) Anderson.
  p.   cm.
 ISBN 0-8054-3013-X
 1. Sunday schools—Growth.   I. Title.
 BV1523.G75A53   1993
 268—dc20                                      92-44805
                                                  CIP

## Dedication

I dedicate this book to the memory of Arthur Flake, on whose "Formula" the Growth Spiral is based . . .

Also, to the thousands of churches whose leaders have used the Growth Spiral and proved that "getting back to the basics" really works in producing growth.

# THE GROWTH SPIRAL
## The Official Interpretation

### GROWTH SPIRAL REPORT

360 Churches ———————— Avg. Involvement — 2 yrs.

| ITEM | BEGIN | NOW | INCREASE | |
|---|---|---|---|---|
| Enr. | 205,551 | 309,273 | 103,722 | 50% |
| Pros. | 78,071 | 181,587 | 103,516 | 133% |
| Units | 9,538 | 14,033 | 4,494 | 47% |
| Workers | 20,163 | 32,817 | 12,654 | 63% |
| WMA | 6,346 | 12,714 | 6,368 | 100% |
| Training | 4,586 | 18,783 | 14,191 | 310% |
| Contacts | 38,501 | 101,445 | 62,944 | 163% |
| Outreaches | 4,836 | 11,645 | 6,809 | 140% |
| SS Att. | 84,704 | 122,489 | 37,785 | 45% |
| WS Att. | 92,771 | 133,253 | 40,482 | 44% |
| Offerings | $1,428,797 | $2,293,043 | $864,246 | 60% |
| Baptisms | 10,309 | 20,119 | 9,810 | 95% |

Andy Anderson

# Contents

# The Growth Spiral

# How the Growth Spiral
# Came to Be

I had already developed the *ACTION Sunday School Enrollment Campaign* before coming to the Baptist Sunday School Board. The program had been adopted for use in the Southern Baptist Convention about a year before I made my move from the local church. Hundreds of churches had used ACTION successfully over many years; others had not experienced success with it. Although I had conducted about two hundred of these programs, I had never seen one fail. However, I stayed in touch with each church long enough to see that it had sufficient teaching units and workers to support its growth.

Before I became a growth specialist at the Baptist Sunday School Board and traveled nationwide, a number of pastors reported to me, "ACTION doesn't work!" I could not understand. Having never seen a program fail, I asked questions: "How many did you enroll?"

"About one hundred."

"How many additional classes did you start?"

"Uh, were we supposed to start some new classes?"

"How many additional workers did you enlist, train and put to work?"

"None."

The problem did not exist with ACTION but with the fact that those churches did not know what to do with the new people when they enrolled them. This was disturbing to me.

My wife and I live in Fort Myers, Florida. For many years we had a small cattle ranch there. Behind the house was a fish pond. I love to fish: cast, fly and cane pole. My favorite is a cane pole. Let me share a small piece of unsolicited advice. If you have a nervous stomach or are concerned about burnout, grab a cane pole and a can of worms, put a cork on the line, and find a place to fish. You cannot watch a cork go under the water and worry at the same time. I am probably alive and healthy today because of cane-pole fishing.

On the bank of the lake there was a log. Now, don't laugh at this. But I call that log my "dialogue." One end of it belongs to the Lord; the other end, to me. On that log I spent many hours "dialoguing" with the Lord.

When I understood the problems we were facing with Sunday School growth, I went to the log and prayed, "Lord, we need guidance. If it meets Your approval, please do not give us another program. We have about all of these we can stand, but we do need help."

I was well aware that the Arthur Flake Formula works. It always has, but I knew I had difficulty using it. Others had expressed the same frustration. Maybe it needed refining. On that log I took a sketch pad and drew designs. I wrote down the five parts of the Flake Formula to see what could be done with them. In the process the Growth Spiral was designed.

I showed it to my pastor, Elmer Crews. "Elmer," I said, "look at this." The young pastor studied it and inquired, "What is it?" I realized then it was not a workable product—back to the "dialogue" again, where I continued to fast and pray for about a year and a half.

One Sunday, following the morning worship service, Elmer and I were talking about the Spiral design. He made a comment which gave an insight and opened the door for the completion of the instrument.

"Andy," he commented, "the Flake Formula is made up of five abstracts: know the prospects, create new teaching units, enlist workers, provide space and visit. I cannot work with abstracts."

I immediately saw the reason why so many people had never used the Formula. They could not make use of abstracts.

I went back to the study. By collecting information and statistics from hundreds of churches, some growing and some not, I developed the formulas to use with the Spiral.

Some of the areas where my study was centered were:

(1) What is the average attrition rate in the Sunday School enrollment?

(2) How many prospects are needed for the enrollment to:
stay the same?
grow 10 percent?
grow 25 percent?
grow 50 percent?
grow 100 percent?

(3) What is the average net-enrollment increase for each additional new class or department? What should be the average size of a teaching unit:
for growing?
for maintenance?

(4) What percent of the enrollment will attend when the worker to enrollment ratio is:

| | |
|---|---|
| 1 to 5? | 1 to 8? |
| 1 to 6? | 1 to 9? |
| 1 to 7? | 1 to 10 or more? |

(5) In order to have a good planning meeting, what percent of the workers need to be present?

(6) How many study course books need to be completed each quarter for the workers to be adequately trained?

(7) How many additional spaces for new classes are needed? How much does a lack of space deter growth? Is it possible to use outside space, and for how long?

(8) How many ministry contacts are necessary each week to meet the needs of the enrollment? Does the number of contacts affect the attendance? If so, how?

(9) How many people must we have in visitation for the program to work?

(10) What percentage of the enrollment can we expect to attend on an average Sunday?

(11) What should be the relationship between the Sunday School attendance and the morning worship service attendance?

(12) What is the best method to determine a church's per capita giving? Is it possible to project the weekly offerings?

(13) How are baptisms affected by:
increased enrollment?
training Sunday School workers as soul-winners?

When I began to study these areas, I realized there were few, if any, statistics in any of them.

I designed a simple, mathematical formula for the Spiral. When it was completed, I asked my pastor to study it again. Within a few moments, he replied, "I can use this. Can we pilot this in our church?" We did.

During the first year, the church grew in Sunday School enrollment from 133 to 399. It was an exciting experience.

But the *quality* of Christian education was better at the end of the year than when we began, even with the large growth. The Sunday School attendance increased from sixty-five to 171. The number of teaching units and workers increased threefold because the enrollment increased 300 percent.

Baptisms increased from three to forty-three—and all of this in one year.

We have continued to refine the Growth Spiral. Today we have an excellent tool which is used by thousands of growing churches.

At the end of each chapter there are statistics from one church which is using the Growth Spiral. These were selected by size and areas of the country. By the time this book is printed, these facts will be out of date since the churches are growing rapidly.

Hundreds of other churches could have been included but, obviously, it would require hundreds of additional pages to record them.

—ANDY

# The Growth Spiral: What Is It?

Some think the Growth Spiral is only a series of numbers, but it is a tool that guides church leadership to plan a more qualitative ministry.

(1) *The Spiral Is Synchronized or Balanced Growth*

You probably know a church which used to be large, probably growing fast. After a while, it decreased rapidly. There is a good chance it grew out of balance. Anything which is out of balance will eventually collapse.

When a church leader emphasizes evangelism and outreach *only*, the church will grow out of balance. It must be balanced with discipleship.

Another leader may emphasize discipleship *only*. The church will fall in the other direction. Discipleship is imperative, but it must be balanced with outreach and evangelism.

Still another leader may place all of the emphasis on constructing new buildings. This, too, is needed. However, the building must be balanced with people. Growing a church in balance is a basic principle. One of the assets of the Spiral is that leaders can see the *relationship* between these factors and keep them balanced.

(2) *The Spiral Is a Controlled Growth Process*

Churches are grown through a process, not a program. This principle is taught in the Bible. "The Lord added to the church *daily* those who were being saved" (Acts 2:47, NKJV, author's italics).

**15**

Every tree, bush, flower and even every blade of grass grows in a process—a little every day. The human body grows in the same manner through a process—a little at a time.

Everything in God's universe grows in a process. Why, then, do we try to grow the church with programs, rapid spurts, high attendance days and special events? All of these are important in the life of the church. However, they are valuable for motivation, not growth. For instance, a high attendance day will produce a lot of excitement and will generate an excellent attendance on a given day, but almost every time the attendance will revert on the following Sunday to the average attendance. By using the same amount of effort in emphasizing the basics of growth, the attendance will increase and remain.

A controlled process is the key to sound church growth.

(3) *The Spiral Is an Evaluation Tool*

In the first chapter of this book I will go into detail about how this instrument guides the leaders to discover where the church is strong and where it is weak. The Spiral reveals: (a) the present conditions; (b) the weak areas; (c) the severity of weaknesses; and (d) a design to correct the problems.

(4) *The Spiral Is a Planning Tool*

It assists in jointly planning several departments of work rather than planning them one at a time. This correlation produces a better balance of planning. This becomes evident as you continue to study the book.

(5) *The Spiral Is a Goal-Setting Tool*

The method used for establishing goals is *the law of cause and effect*. This law is operative in every part of the universe and is equally effective in the church.

A good goal is valuable. A bad goal is demoralizing. The church's present Sunday School and worship attendance, the offerings and the baptisms are the result of what the church is presently doing (the law of cause and effect).

When the items that produce growth are increased, we are able to predict the growth. This method becomes evident in the following chapter.

(6)  *The Spiral Is an Administrative Tool*

Church leaders are about as busy as they can be. They do not need another program. Several surveys show that when the Spiral is correctly used, a leader can save as much as 50 percent of his or her time in administering the Sunday School program.

The material in this book will: assist you to understand the Growth Spiral; develop a Growth Spiral for your church; and give you the "how to" to reach, teach, evangelize and disciple every person in your church field.

### CALVARY BAPTIST CHURCH
*Beaumont, TX*

| ITEM | APR. '83 | OCT. '90 | INCREASE |
|---|---|---|---|
| Enrollment | 718 | 3,441 | 2,723 |
| Prospects | 780 | 2,600 | 1,820 |
| Teaching Units | 45 | 178 | 142 |
| Workers | 88 | 453 | 365 |
| Workers' Mtng. Att. | 32 | 210 | 178 |
| Training Awards | 40 | 774 | 734 |
| Weekly Contacts | 110 | 2,100 | 1,990 |
| Outreachers | 45 | 175 | 135 |
| SS Attendance | 357 | 1,223 | 866 |
| WS Attendance | 395 | 1,514 | 1,119 |
| Weekly Offerings | $7,318 | $31,300 | $23,982 |
| Baptisms | 14 | 218 | 204 |

# 1

# The Value of Evaluation

In the back of the book you will find a *completed* Sunday School Growth Spiral. Look at and follow it during the reading of this chapter.

This is a sample Spiral, a teaching Spiral, not an actual church. This example is used in my conferences throughout the world.

## Date

First, there is the Date column. You will notice in the first block I have placed the date of the beginning of the church year—10/1, October 1.

Above this date, the year is divided into four quarters—1/1, 4/1, 7/1, and back to 10/1. It is easier to reach a quarter goal than an annual goal.

## Enrollment

Next, notice that the enrollment is 200. Later, when you develop your own Spiral, you will place your church's Sunday School enrollment in this location. *Do not fill in your Spiral now.*

I have placed a plus mark beside the enrollment. This is the evaluation. If the Sunday School enrollment is larger than it was one year ago, it is growing numerically and receives a plus. However, if the enrollment is the same or less than it was a year ago, it will receive a minus.

This is an elementary evaluation tool, but it is valuable as it helps us to determine whether or not we are growing, maintaining, or declining. This is the primary reason for starting our study with the enrollment column.

Later, we will see how to increase the enrollment.

## Prospects

The next column is labeled Prospects. Notice that there are sixty-five prospects at this time.

This is the result of adding two groups together: *every unenrolled, resident church member; other prospects on file.* Added together, there are sixty-five prospects.

There is a minus by this column, indicating that there are not enough prospects.

Surveys have shown that we need at least as many prospects for enrollment as we have people who are enrolled. Because there are two hundred enrolled and only sixty-five prospects, a minus has been recorded.

One of the primary reasons for nongrowth is a lack of valid prospects.

## Teaching Units

In the adult- and youth-age groups, we call the teaching units classes. In the children- and preschool-age groups we call the teaching unit a department.

Since I am referring to all of the age groups, I cannot use either "class" or "department" here. Therefore, the words *teaching unit* are descriptive. A teaching unit is a group of students and a teacher.

Having counted the number of teaching units in the Sunday School, I place an 8 in the block. Now do some math. We need to discover the ratio of teaching units to the enrollment; therefore, we divide 8 into 200. The result is 25.

The interpretation is: on an average, twenty-five people are enrolled in each teaching unit. Obviously, some of the units have more than twenty-five enrolled while others have less, but the average is twenty-five.

This number is not too large for maintenance, but it is too large for growth. Once classes reach this size, they cease to grow. The teacher has more people than he or she can minister to and, as a result, does not desire to reach others. There are exceptions to this rule, though.

We are not interested in organizing a Sunday School merely to care for the status quo. We are concerned about creating enough teaching units to reach the unreached. Therefore, this sample church needs additional classes and departments. Notice there is a minus for the evaluation.

The best size for growth seems to be an average enrollment between twelve and eighteen. Many of the small churches have an average enrollment of six, eight or ten. When about one-half of the enrollment attends on a given Sunday, it is possible that the attendance in individual classes is so small the teaching unit will die by itself. These small units need to be "fleshed out," enlarged, by enrolling more people. It seems that the best ratio for a teaching unit is an enrollment of between twelve and eighteen. The unit is large enough so it does not die by itself, yet it is small enough to grow.

Before we dig more deeply into this part of the study, realize that this book is designed to assist you in developing a Spiral for *the whole church* and Spirals for *each age group in the Sunday School.* You need to develop a Spiral for each class and department because the ratios are considerably different in each. This study is found in chapters 15 through 18.

## Workers

Here is the list of those counted as workers on the Spiral. Other people work in the Sunday School, but these are the ones counted in this ratio.

(1) Class teachers
(2) Class outreach leaders
(3) Department directors
(4) Department outreach/evangelism leaders
(5) Pastor
(6) Minister of Education (if you have one)
(7) Other church-staff people who work in the Sunday School
(8) General outreach/evangelism director

(9)  Sunday School director
(10)  Adult group (care) leaders
If you have a division Sunday School, include:
(11)  Division directors
(12)  Division outreach/evangelism directors

In the sample Sunday School, there are eighteen workers. This number is placed in the Workers block. We are ready for another evaluation. Divide the number of workers into the enrollment. The result shows one worker for every eleven people enrolled in the Sunday School. Here is another minus. We should have a worker for every five people enrolled in Sunday School. There is a need for additional workers, but, until they are enlisted, there is a serious problem. This will be discussed in chapter 5.

## Workers' Meeting

Look at the block labeled Workers' Meeting on the sample Spiral. Some churches have a weekly meeting, some monthly, and others, quarterly. There is an average attendance of six people in my workers' meeting and a minus beside the block.

In order to earn a plus in this column there ought to be at least 75 percent of the workers in attendance, a large percentage. It is possible to have a *meeting* without that many people in attendance, but this is a *planning meeting*, and we need to have at least three-fourths of the workers participating. With six workers out of eighteen in attendance, we do not have our quota, a minus.

*The workers' meeting, in my estimation, is the most important meeting in the church.* You would probably expect a minister of education to say that, but I am at heart a pastor. *If we use this meeting correctly, it will revolutionize the church. If we use this meeting incorrectly, we will continue to limp along without sufficient quantity, quality, or power.* This is not to state that a church should have this meeting instead of a worship service. Rather it is to emphasize that we will have a larger, more effective and powerful worship service if the Sunday School leadership correctly plans once a week. Plans are made to increase attendance, improve quality Bible teaching and ministry, and reach the unsaved. The workers pray for, by name, those who are being reached and work with the pastor in evangelizing and discipling them. These are some of the activities that are accomplished when the workers' meeting is carried out correctly.

In chapter 6 the workers' meeting will be discussed in detail.

When I was a young pastor, I was constantly concerned about the quantity and quality of the Sunday School and worship service. Each Saturday night I would spend time wondering about how many people would be present the next morning. Sleepless Saturday nights came and went, but when I learned the value of the workers' meeting, matters changed.

I assembled the Sunday School leadership on Wednesday evening. They were the best-trained, most-dedicated people in the church. They formed an army of associates. I said to them, "I love and appreciate you. I need you. Will you help me get the job done?" They went to work, and I went to sleep on Saturday night. Never again did I worry about the attendance or the quality, because there was an organized, praying, visiting, motivated group working with me. Church leaders could benefit from realizing the value of this meeting.

### Training Awards

The next block on the sample Spiral is labeled Training Awards. *A training award is the completion of a study course book.*

The training awards that we count in the Spiral are the study course books which were completed during the last three months and which related to Sunday School work. This is a quarter, a three-month block.

For example, my wife and I attended a conference center. We each received one training award. Those were the only two in our church during the last quarter, so I placed 2 in the block on the sample Spiral.

You will notice that there is a minus. In order to garner a plus, the number of training awards each quarter must equal at least one-half of the number of workers. There are eighteen workers; therefore, at least nine training awards should have been earned this quarter.

Why is this goal set so high? None of us would allow our children to attend a public school where the teachers had no specialized training. Yet, we are visiting in our community, inviting, "Come to our Sunday School. Our teachers don't have any training, but the Holy Spirit is with them." But even the Holy Spirit cannot bring back to our memory that which we have never learned. There is a profound need for an increase in training.

One of the reasons for the success of the Spiral is it offers a specific plan to produce quality equal to quantity. There is an emphasis on finding and enrolling people, but there is an equal emphasis on producing a quality Bible-teaching/ministering program.

## Space

There are eight teaching units, and each of them meets in a space, of course. After doing a "space walk" throughout the building, we discover a few more places where classes can meet. In fact, there are four more spaces. Eight spaces are being used, plus four that can be used, accounting for twelve spaces. So the number 12 is in the block labeled Space on the sample Spiral.

On the sample Spiral there is a plus. If there is at least one more space not being used, we have a plus. Big deal! Yet, a church is in a serious condition if it has no space for future growth.

## Contacts

*A contact is a personal visit, a card or letter, or a telephone call.*

On the sample Spiral, it is recorded that the members are making sixty contacts a week. However, there is a minus. The weekly contacts need to equal at least one-half of the enrollment. Why? Because approximately one-half of the enrollment is absent each week. The least a church can do is to contact these to see if a ministry needs to be performed. Contacts are valuable ministries.

## Outreachers

*An outreacher is one who makes personal visits. One who is writing cards/letters or making telephone calls is not considered an outreacher in this category—only those involved in the visitation program.* Some may not visit on the assigned day and time. However, they should be counted in the total.

A minus is placed for the evaluation. In order to receive a plus, there should be at least one person in outreach for each teaching unit. There are eight teaching units—thus the need for a minimum of eight outreachers each week.

A class or department is not functioning properly if it is not meeting the ministry needs of its members who are absent.

## Sunday School Attendance

Now, let us continue to work around the sample Spiral. The average Sunday School attendance is seventy-five.

Divide the Sunday School enrollment into the Sunday School attendance. This allows us to find the percentage of enrollment that attends.

Seventy-five is the attendance; two hundred is the enrollment. The math reveals that the average attendance is only 38 percent of the enrollment.

If the Sunday School attendance is between 40 and 60 percent of the enrollment, it is acceptable.

The type of community in which a church is located has an impact on the average attendance. If located in a rural setting, the attendance is usually higher than if it is located in a resort area, for example.

It is suggested that the leadership of the church make a profile study to discover what the average percentage has been over the previous five to ten years.

Divide the enrollment into the attendance each year for the last several years. Most churches discover that approximately the same percentage has prevailed. This is true unless there has been a large, unsuccessful ACTION program or there has been a major cleaning of the Sunday School rolls.

If the average attendance is below 40 percent of the enrollment, the church earns a minus. There is a minus on the sample Spiral because the attendance is 38 percent.

If the attendance is 60 percent of the enrollment or larger, a minus is given. This is because it is almost impossible to retain 60 percent or more in average attendance unless someone is purging the Sunday School roll.

I was once asked by a co-worker why we have to settle for about 50 percent of the enrollment in attendance each week. Think with me for a moment.

On a given Sunday add together the following: those who are out of town; those who are working at a secular vocation; those who are ill; those who attend the sick; and those who are backslidden.

The simple logistics of a congregation keep us from having more than about one-half of the enrollment on a Sunday. This does not mean that only one-half of the members attend Sunday School, because over a few weeks almost all of them are present at least once.

We should never be satisfied with the attendance. A more detailed study of the attendance is considered in a later chapter.

Carefully study the evaluations on the sample Spiral. *If the average attendance is less than 40 percent of the enrollment there are weaknesses.* What are the weaknesses on the sample church? *Every place there is a minus there is a weakness.* Once we have identified these, we can correct them.

If the average attendance is 60 percent or larger, attention should be given to controlling the enrollment.

## Worship Service Attendance

Now we consider the morning worship service attendance. There are eighty-five people in attendance on the sample Spiral. Notice that the evaluation is a plus.

The Sunday School attendance and the worship service attendance should be within 10 percent of each other to be the best. There needs to be a balance between worship and Sunday School. Christians need to worship but they also need to study.

If the pastor is a dynamic, charismatic leader, his drawing power will develop a large, meaningful worship hour. He should lead the worshipers into the Bible Study hour. Likewise, if the Bible Study program is extremely strong, it should feed the worship hour.

## Offerings

In the block labeled Offerings I have placed $750. This is the total weekly, undesignated offering. Notice the word *total*. Some of the offerings come through the Sunday School, the worship service, the mail, and on Wednesday night.

If a church receives enough money to pay its bills, it receives a plus. But if there is not enough money to pay the bills, there will be a minus. The chapter on church finances shows how a church can have all of the money required to do all it needs to do.

## Baptisms

The column labeled Baptisms is an *annual* block. In order to complete this statistic, we had to examine the church records to see how many people were baptized each year over the last several years. *The average per year is the figure placed here.* The average number of baptisms for the sample church is three per year. Notice that I have a ? for the evaluation. This is awfully difficult to evaluate. If you believe the church is doing all it ought to do in the field of evangelism, then give yourself a plus. Otherwise, you need to consider a minus.

We have completed our circle around the Spiral and evaluated each feature. Now we come to another valuable characteristic.

## Why Do We Have These Areas?

Observe again the four projections on the sample Spiral: Sunday School Attendance, Worship Attendance, Offerings and Baptisms.

Why do we have these four statistics?

A man in one of my conferences commented, "I don't know why we have these statistics, but they're the same figures we've had since I've been in the church for over thirty years, so I guess that's what we're supposed to have."

No, no, no! These four statistics are simply the result of the other items on the Spiral: Enrollment, Prospects, Units, Workers, Workers' Meeting Attendance, Training, Space, Contacts and Outreachers.

This is the law of cause and effect. We are not robots! But if we increase the enrollment, prospects, workers, units, training, planning, outreach ministry—then the attendance, offerings, and evangelism increase accordingly. If we decrease the enrollment, combine teaching units, and the like, the attendance, offerings and evangelism decrease.

The law of cause and effect, God's law, works better in the church than in other places.

## What Does the Growth Spiral Reveal to Us?

(1)  First, what is really going on in our church. Most of us are not familiar with some of the more important factors in church growth.

(2)  Second, the weaknesses as well as strengths in the church. The Spiral is designed to help us change every minus into a plus during the year.

(3)  Third, the words, *Sunday School Growth Spiral* are written on the sample Spiral. But this is not just a Sunday School program.

*The Spiral Is a Church Program:*

(a)  The first two columns on the Spiral—*enrollment* and *prospects*—are the church's outreach program.

(b)  *Units* represent the church's organizational program.

(c)  *Workers, workers' meeting,* and *training* contain the church's discipleship program.

(d)  *Space* is the church's building program.

(e)  *Contacts* and *outreachers* are the church's ministry programs.

(f)  *Sunday School attendance* is the church's Bible teaching program.

(g)  *Worship attendance* is the church's worship program.

(h)  *Offerings* is the church's stewardship program.

(i)  *Baptisms* is the church's evangelism program.

The Growth Spiral is designed to measure balanced growth. A church can grow at any speed it desires. If it remains in balance, at the end of one, two, five or even ten years, it will have a better Christian education program than it has now.

(4)  Look again at the sample Spiral.

At the top, is the word *Quantity*; next, the word *Quality*, and at the bottom of the page you will see the word *Ministry*. On this tripod you can build a strong church. The Growth Spiral will help you balance quantity, quality and ministry.

## Resources

There are a couple of resources that will help guide your church to reach, teach and minister to the people in your church, community, and world.

(1) Videotapes on the Growth Spiral are available for purchase by calling 1-800/458-BSSB, or by computer from E.C.O.S. (Easy Church Order System), CIS, 127 9th Ave. N., Nashville, TN 37234.

Leaders of the Baptist Sunday School Board asked me to make these videos. They are helpful to a church which desires to use the Spiral effectively.

(2) You may also be interested in purchasing the *Sunday School Growth Spiral Promotion Packet*. This packet is filled with charts, banners, and other items. There is a wall-size Spiral, like the sample Spiral included in this book. Enrollment, contact, visitation, attendance and training awards records are included. It can also be purchased from the Nashville, Tennessee, address. The Growth Spiral will help you to plan, promote, set goals, and motivate your people.

### LAKEWAY BAPTIST CHURCH
*The Colony, TX*

| ITEM | JAN. '87 | OCT. '90 | INCREASE |
|---|---|---|---|
| Enrollment | 58 | 709 | 651 |
| Prospects | 35 | 650 | 615 |
| Teaching Units | 7 | 46 | 39 |
| Workers | 14 | 70 | 56 |
| Workers' Mtng. Att. | NA | 35 | 35 |
| Training Awards | NA | 12 | 12 |
| Weekly Contacts | 50 | 200 | 150 |
| Outreachers | 6 | 10 | 4 |
| SS Attendance | 56 | 313 | 257 |
| WS Attendance | 75 | 370 | 295 |
| Weekly Offerings | $840 | $3,375 | $2,535 |
| Baptisms | 0 | 50 | 50 |

# The Church's Outreach Ministry

*The Value of Enrollment*
*The Value of Prospects*

The local church has a responsibility to discover every prospect who lives in the church field. It is impossible to reach the people unless they are first identified.

An aggressive enrollment emphasis is needed to reach a maximum number of prospects.

# 2

# The Value of Enrollment

## Review

There are two hundred people enrolled in the sample Sunday School. After checking the record, I discover there are more people enrolled now than a year ago; the evaluation is a plus.

There are sixty-five prospects. That is not enough—record a minus. There are not enough workers—again, a minus. Attendance at the planning meeting is weak, and the training awards are below normal—two more minuses. Yet, there is enough space for continued growth—give it a plus.

The contact ministry is weak, and there are not enough people involved in the outreach program—two more minuses.

Though we have a good Sunday School attendance, it is not what it should be—again, a minus.

The offerings are sufficient to pay the bills—a plus. The evangelism is rather good but not good enough.

## Develop a Growth Spiral for Your Church

You will find a blank Spiral in the back of this book. Place the dates of the quarters in the blanks. Fill in the blanks as you continue to study the book.

## Open Enrollment Versus Traditional Methods

Many church leaders believe that prospects should attend the Sunday School three Sundays in succession before enrolling. As far as I know, this has never been the policy in any denominational manual.

Such a misconception has been developed through tradition. There was a time when the quality of a Sunday School was measured by the percentage of the enrollment in attendance. This forced the class membership to screen the new attendants to be sure they would be faithful. Otherwise, their lack of faithfulness would lower the class percentage. It also resulted in removing from the roll those who were not regular in attendance.

We need to reconsider these basic methods of enrollment and compare them to the open method of enrollment—*enroll anyone, anywhere, at any time, if they agree to being enrolled.*

### Enroll Anyone Versus Attending Three Sundays

Traditionally, we do not enroll a person until they have attended the class session for three successive Sundays. This is appalling in that Christians are instructed to go into the highways, hedges, streets, and lanes, and to compel them to come in. We are unwilling to really accept a person into our membership until they prove they will be regular in attendance. This is unscriptural.

But there is another reason why this seems to be irregular: we will accept, joyfully, into the church membership a person who attends the first Sunday. Open enrollment invites us to enroll anyone. We should be willing to enroll a person even before he or she attends the class session. For instance, we are participating in the church visitation program on Monday night. We visit a family that has just moved into our community. They express a desire to join the Sunday School. Is it improper to enroll them before they attend?

### Enroll Anywhere Versus Enroll in the Classroom

With many churches the only place you can enroll a person is in the classroom. This is because the roll book is opened only in this room. It is almost impossible to enroll in the hall, department room, or even in the sanctuary because the class record book is not opened there. Tradition limits the enrollment activity in a church.

The open enrollment method is simple. When we discover some-one who wants to enroll, we enroll them wherever they are. This unties the hands of the Christians to do the work of God outside of the church building.

*Enroll at Any Time Versus Enroll on Sunday*

Traditionally, the only time you could enroll people in Sunday School was on Sunday morning because it was the only time the record books were open. If you tried to enroll before Sunday School started or after the class secretary finished the records, it was impossible.

Open enrollment gives us the opportunity to enroll people any time of the day or night—twenty-four hours a day.

*Summary*

*Traditionally* we enrolled: those who attended three Sundays; in the classroom; while the class record books were open.

*Open Enrollment*, we enroll: anyone who desires to be a member; anywhere; anytime. Open Enrollment is biblical.

You may or may not agree with the next statement, but give me an opportunity to explain it.

*The Sunday School enrollment is the most important statistic in the church. It is more important than the attendance, the offerings, and even more important than baptisms because, to a large degree, it controls these items.* In the next few pages I will discuss these one at a time and share with you certain strong convictions that have come from a lifetime of experience.

Enrollment is valuable because:

1. *At the moment of enrollment, ministry begins.* We rarely do minister to prospects. In fact, most of us do not even know who they are. We minister to people who are enrolled in our Sunday School.

People are enrolled not for what they can do for us but for what we can do for them. When a person enrolls, the class becomes responsible. It cares for the person, visits him (her), witnesses to him, disciples him, etc. Ministry begins at the time of enrollment. That is a valuable reason for us to enroll people in Bible study.

2. *Attendance is controlled by the enrollment.* Both the Sunday School and worship service attendance are controlled, to a considerable degree, by the Sunday School enrollment.

Since the average attendance is between 40 and 60 percent of the enrollment, it stands to reason that if the enrollment increases, the attendance will increase. If the enrollment decreases, the attendance will decrease. The Sunday School enrollment strongly influences attendance. To a large extent, Sunday School attendance controls worship service turnout. When people attend Sunday School they usually remain for the worship service. Every study shows that the two attendances increase or decrease together.

3. *Offerings are controlled by the enrollment.* The enrollment controls the attendance. The attendance controls the offerings. So, the enrollment is more important than the offering.

If the enrollment is not increased, the attendance will not increase, and the offerings will be about the same next year as they are now. Later in this book when we discuss the offerings you will discover how we make the projection so that *you can have all of the money that you need in your church.*

4. *Baptisms are affected by the enrollment.* Here is why. When we use open enrollment (anyone, anywhere, anytime if they agree) about one-half of the people we enroll will be the unsaved.

If we do not enroll additional lost people in Sunday School, of course we will not have lost people around the church. Studies show that most of the unsaved will be saved and baptized within twelve months from the time of their enrollment. If the enrollment does not increase, evangelism will decrease because most of the unsaved in the Sunday School will have received Christ. Thus, increasing the enrollment is imperative for evangelism to continue.

### The Value of Enrollment

1. Ministry begins at enrollment.
2. Sunday School attendance is controlled by enrollment.
3. Worship service attendance is controlled by enrollment.

4. Offerings are controlled by enrollment.

5. Baptisms are affected by enrollment.

These five imperatives make us realize how valuable enrollment is.

*Five Methods to Enroll People in Bible Study*

Churches with whom I work in the Spiral use these five specific methods to enroll people in Sunday School. In the last report, the average church employing these methods had a *net* enrollment gain of 154 during the year. The other churches who were not using these methods, however, had a net gain of one during the same time. There are no gimmicks—only five basic methods for enrolling people in Sunday School. I believe that any church, using these methods *every* week, can achieve amazing results.

1. *Enroll people who are visiting in the Sunday School classroom.* This question was asked in a survey: "Will you enroll a person in Sunday School the first Sunday they attend?" Seventy-one percent replied, "No." That is appalling. A subquestion was, "If not, why not?" The answer was. "What if they don't return?" Isn't that interesting? The Bible instructs us to go into the highways, hedges, streets, and lanes, and *compel* them to come in. When we finally get them to attend, we won't enroll them because they may not come back. That doesn't sound too Christian. They should be invited to enroll while they are in the Sunday School classroom. This shows the newcomer that he or she is wanted in our fellowship.

The registration card many of our churches use is in reality a visitor's card. Everyone at Sunday School is encouraged to complete some kind of card, so we give the guest a visitor's card. By the way, would you consider deleting the word *visitor* from your church vocabulary? *Visitor* sort of means "you're not within our circle." I encourage you to use the word *guest*. When you call a person a *guest*, you imply, "You're a part of us." It's a far better word.

What do we normally say when we give the guest a card? "Joe, we're glad to have you visiting with us. Would you fill out this card, please?" Joe completes it. Why don't we give him an enrollment card?

I asked a class secretary that question one Sunday morning after he presented a visitor's card to a guest. He answered, "Well, he isn't a member, so he must be a visitor."

I encourage you to discard the visitor's cards and purchase *enrollment cards*. They are Form 10 on the Broadman Supplies order blank. Use them in your Sunday School classes. They may be purchased from a Christian bookstore or by calling 1/800/458-BSSB.

Many of the people who are guests in the Sunday School classes will enroll when given an opportunity. If the guests cannot enroll, instruct them to write the word *guest* on the card. How many people would you have enrolled last Sunday if this card had been used in the classes?

2. *Enroll people in the worship service.* Most churches use some type of card to register the attendance of those who visit in their worship services. Let me encourage you to place one more line on that card. "Enroll me in Sunday School," followed by a place for them to check. As they participate in the worship service, they can also enroll in the Sunday School.

Let me give you an illustration. I was visiting in an Oklahoma church. When the Sunday School report was given during the morning worship service, it revealed that there were many more people in the auditorium than were in Sunday School. We distributed enrollment cards to everyone in the service.

I asked: "If you are a member of a Sunday School class, please reenroll. Help us verify phone numbers, addresses, and other information. If you are not enrolled in Sunday School, we want you to enroll now." The result of that effort was that sixty-three new people enrolled in Sunday School during that service.

An interesting part of this story was that a lady came by afterwards and said, "Thank you, Dr. Anderson, for letting me join the Sunday School. I have been trying for seven years to join!" We have almost locked the doors in order to protect the enrollment.

A person may attend the worship service, respond to the invitation, and join our church on the first Sunday he attends. And yet, many of our churches are still demanding that people attend the

Sunday School three Sundays in succession before they allow them to join the Sunday School.

Even if we do not use this outmoded plan, we overlook the fact that we should invite them to enroll.

The Bible instructs us to *compel* them to come in, and *the most compelling force in the world is love.* We need to say to the people, "We want you to become a part of our family *today.*" That speaks volumes. Enroll people during the worship services.

3. *Use the "Application for Church Membership" card to enroll people in Sunday School.*—These cards are already used in many churches. This is a Broadman Supplies product and can be purchased from a Christian bookstore or ordered by calling 1/800/458-BSSB. The cards are usually kept on clipboards and placed on the front pew in the auditorium. If you do not use this card, include this information on your card: "When a person joins the church, they are requested to fill out the card."

There is nothing on this card about joining the Sunday School. Can you imagine? Allowing people to join our church and not letting them join our Sunday School. And do you know what the major argument is? "They have never attended Sunday School, so they can't join." We need to reexamine what the church is. It is more than a worship service. Shouldn't we enroll them in our Sunday School when they unite with our church family? Sam Jones joins our church. We receive him into our church membership, but we do not have a practical method to enroll him in Sunday School. What kind of follow-up takes place after he joins the church? Probably none, even though we plan for it. The back door of our church is wide open, and people are going straight through.

There are three actions used when people join the church:

1. Do nothing about enrolling the new person into the Sunday School.
2. Automatically enroll everyone who joins the church. This is better than doing nothing, but the new member is given no choice.
3. Place one more line on the *Application for Church Membership* card you use: Enroll me in Sunday School _____.

Already Enrolled: Yes _____, No _____. Now when Joe joins the church, he *voluntarily* enrolls in the Sunday School. Immediately, Joe is surrounded by a teacher and a group of men who will love and disciple him.

These three enrollment opportunities are *inside* the church: Enroll people in Sunday School; enroll people in the worship service; enroll people when they join the church.

If you had used these three methods last Sunday, how many would you have enrolled in Sunday School? Most churches would see a dramatic increase in the enrollment without going outside the church. When we open our arms and invite people to join us in Bible Study, it is amazing what will happen. Once these people are enrolled, love them and meet their needs. About one-half of them will attend each week. Some of them will never attend, but we will be able to meet their spiritual needs because someone has the responsibility for their nurture.

However, we must also go *outside* of the church building. This brings us to the fourth enrollment method.

4. *Use the Enrollment Kit.* The *Enrollment Kit* is probably the finest single enrollment idea in existence. Inside the Kit are enrollment cards. They are about the size of calling cards. They can be purchased from an area Christian bookstore, by calling 1-800/458-BSSB, or by computer from E.C.O.S. (Easy Church Order System), CIS, 127 9th Ave. N., Nashville, TN 37234.

This is a valuable tool. It is hard to enroll people without cards. The kit is the right size to fit nicely into a pocket or purse so you will have the cards in your possession at all times.

Let me give you an illustration. One of our churches provided these cards for the people in their church. A high school senior girl took her packet and between Sundays enrolled fifty-three of her classmates in Sunday School. How could she do this? She had enrollment cards. Again, it is hard to enroll people without cards. Church members need to be equipped with these tools.

Members are not instructed to go up and down the street enrolling people. (That is the method used in *ACTION, A Sunday School Enrollment Program* which can be purchased by calling 1/800/458-

BSSB.) They are encouraged to enroll family, friends, neighbors, business associates, schoolmates, etc. The response can be overwhelming.

Now, examine the fifth method of enrolling people in Sunday School.

5. *Use Enrollment Kits during the visitation program.* Equip the people who participate in the visitation program with *Enrollment Kits.* This makes it possible for them to enroll prospects when they visit.

Dr. Fran Terhune, minister of Education, Westside Baptist Church, Gainesville, Florida, stated in a conference that the participants in their weekly visitation program are equipped with *Enrollment Kits.* In one year, the visitation teams enrolled over five hundred people.

These are not gimmicks. They are basic processes which enable us to share our love and the love of our Lord. The result is that the Sunday School enrollment may increase significantly.

The above five methods should be practiced weekly.

The following two methods are used annually.

1. *Transfer Plan (for Vacation Bible School).* On the closing Saturday morning of the Vacation Bible School, enlist the VBS workers plus teachers of the Sunday School preschool and children's departments to visit from 10:00 to noon. The purpose is to obtain permission from the parents to transfer the records of the unenrolled children to the Sunday School roll. Thus, we enroll them in the ongoing Bible teaching program of the church. When we calendar this event, it will occur.

Also, why not have a banquet for the Vacation Bible School workers to be served at noon on this Saturday? This is an excellent opportunity to say thank you to these faithful workers

2. *A Mini-ACTION program.* This ACTION program is one of the most successful enrollment programs in church history when done correctly, yet it is too aggressive for many churches.

After studying the material, decide to use it in a controlled situation. Make a list of prospects and try to enroll them during a Sunday afternoon of visitation.

At the beginning of this chapter, I stated that your Sunday School enrollment is the most important statistic in your church. If it is, then use practical, efficient methods to increase it.

Now return to the Spiral and see how it guides in establishing enrollment goals. Notice that the annual goal in the Enrollment column on the sample Spiral is 252. We establish a process by which the enrollment increases by a *net* gain of one person per week. Keep in mind that this is a *net* gain. There is a difference between a *gross* gain and a *net* gain. We may enroll five people on Sunday, and yet net only one because we remove four from the roll for some reason. We set a goal for a *net* gain of one person a week. The Spiral is developed one quarter at a time.

We have two hundred enrolled in October. By January 1, thirteen weeks later, we will have 213, one new member a week net gain. In the next quarter we continue to have a net increase of one person per week, which nets thirteen more. The goal for six months is 226. If we continue at this same pace for the next quarter, we will have 239 people enrolled, and by the end of the year, 252. This has been accomplished by increasing the enrollment a net gain of one person a week.

If we have a net gain of two people per week, we would enroll twenty-six people a quarter, and by the end of the year, the enrollment would increase from two hundred to 304.

It is not difficult to assimilate people into our fellowship when we enroll them like this; therefore, they will be more faithful in attendance. If you enroll too many people at one time and do not have enough teachers, classes, or ministries to care for them, you will lose many. The Spiral helps keep us in balance.

There is another method for setting an enrollment goal which has proven to be challenging and yet adequate. Encourage each teaching unit to have a *net* enrollment increase of one new member each quarter. This results in a *net* increase of four for each class/department each year. Multiply this by the number of teaching units, and this becomes the annual *net* enrollment goal. This is very effective because all of the workers participate in the growth.

*The Bonsai Tree*

I have a fascinating tree. Even though it is small, it is a tree. It is called a bonsai tree. If this tree had been left alone in nature, it probably would be too large to be placed in a building because this species grows to immense size. This tree is several years old and it is no taller than my hand.

How do they keep this tree from growing large? Periodically, someone removes it from its container, clips off some of its roots, and replants it, being careful not to kill it. *They remove enough roots to keep it from growing but leave enough roots for it to live.* This is what happens in many of our Sunday Schools. *The enrollment is the root system of the Sunday School.*

Periodically, someone pulls up the Sunday School records, cleans the roll, and replants the Sunday School, leaving just enough enrollment for it to live, but not enough for it to grow.

Remember the bonsai tree when someone suggests that the Sunday School roll should be purged. Churches are dying or merely staying alive because of the cleaning of their rolls.

The common consensus seems to be that we should remove a name from the Sunday School roll when the enrollee does not attend over a period of time. But, look at the tragedy. Who are the first people we remove from the Sunday School rolls for non-attendance? The unsaved! They have no allegiance to God, to the Bible, or to the church, so they do not attend. *The priority of the Sunday School is evangelism. But, if we remove from our rolls the evangelistic prospects, we are defeating the purpose of the church.*

*Increase the enrollment!* Major on enrollment; do not major on percentage. *God never placed us in a percentage business, but He did put us in a people business.* Build quality and ministry into the educational program, and watch God perform miracles. I repeat: the Sunday School enrollment is the most important statistic in the church.

It is now time for you to decide on an enrollment goal for your church. How much net gain do you think your church can increase *each week?* Multiply this number by 13. Add this number to your present enrollment and place the total in the first quarter block.

Multiply the weekly net gain by 26, add it to the present enrollment, and place it in the next quarter's block. Do it again by multiplying the number by 39 and by 52 in order to complete the column.

Enrollment is not the only ingredient in church growth, as the Growth Spiral reveals, but it is extremely important.

### CAMERON BAPTIST CHURCH
*Lawton, OK*

| ITEM | APR. '82 | JUNE '90 | INCREASE |
|---|---|---|---|
| Enrollment | 1,320 | 3,046 | 1,726 |
| Prospects | 500 | 2,650 | 2,150 |
| Teaching Units | 54 | 135 | 81 |
| Workers | 121 | 334 | 213 |
| Workers' Mtng. Att. | 60 | 234 | 174 |
| Training Awards | 12 | 150 | 138 |
| Weekly Contacts | 888 | 2,320 | 1,432 |
| Outreachers | 54 | 310 | 256 |
| SS Attendance | 539 | 995 | 456 |
| WS Attendance | 550 | 965 | 415 |
| Weekly Offerings | $4,400 | $13,033 | $9,533 |
| Baptisms | 200 | 200 | |

# 3

# The Value of Prospects

In the last chapter we discovered the value of Sunday School enrollment and how to increase it. In this chapter we now turn our attention to prospects. Notice that we have already filled in the Prospects block on the sample Spiral with 65, but we need a number equal to the enrollment.

By the end of the first quarter with 213 people enrolled, we will need 213 prospects. Rarely can a church secure all of the prospects it needs by the end of the first quarter, but establish a large goal and try to reach it. By the end of six months, with 226 people enrolled in Sunday School, we hope to have 226 prospects. This continues with 239 prospects at the end of nine months, and 252 prospects by the end of the year. We place a strong emphasis on prospects. Normally, churches do not place much emphasis on this vital facet of our work.

Most Sunday Schools are organized only to care for the people who are enrolled. Arthur Flake, the genius of Sunday School and church growth in the last generation, instructed us to take a census and find out how many people in the community are unreached. Discover who they are, where they live, their gender, age and their school grade. Gather this information, tabulate it, enlarge the organization, and go after the people.

*It is impossible for a church to grow without enough valid prospects.* When we exhaust the prospects, we have no one to enroll, no one to win, and, therefore, we go into a maintenance mode. Many churches have ceased to grow because they have no valid prospects. A pastor was asked, "How many prospects do you have?" He answered, "Oh, thousands of them." The consultant asked, "Where do you keep all those names?" The pastor opened the window in his study, looked out over the city, and commented, "There they are, thousands of prospects." That is not what I am talking about.

In order for a prospect to be valid, we need a name, an address, an age, a gender, a phone number, and, if possible, school grade and church or church-organization relationship. Hopefully, we also collect information about their native language, in case we need a special class.

Even more important is that the prospect must be *assigned* to the teaching unit which is responsible for reaching and ministry.

We need to: discover those we ought to reach; organize the Sunday School to reach them; assign every prospect to the class or department which is responsible; and begin a visitation ministry.

The number of valid prospects can determine the rate of growth. Let me give you the summary of several surveys: when prospects equal one-half the enrollment, a church can grow about 25 percent a year; when prospects equal the enrollment, a church can grow about 50 percent a year; when prospects equal twice the enrollment, a church can grow about 100 percent a year.

I am not saying that a church will grow 25, 50, or 100 percent in a given year if they have that many prospects, but the study shows that this will be the maximum a church can grow because it will run out of prospects.

What is the maximum number of prospects a church should have? Our studies show that if you have prospects equal to twice the Sunday School enrollment, you have all of the prospects you need at one given time. Beyond that number, the prospects will become invalid before you can work with them. In most cases prospects become invalid if they are not ministered to within three months. They change their minds, move or join another church.

### Here Are Some Effective Methods for Prospecting

(1) I developed another card which is most effective. We call it the *Who Do Card*. It will grab attention quicker than the other. The name comes from the sentence "Who do you know that is a prospect for our Sunday School?"

Here is what churches are discovering: If there are one hundred people in the room and you give each a card, you will receive about seventy-five responses. These are the best prospects we can garner because they are referrals. They are not suspects—they are prospects! Also, we find that we can use the card once a month, because almost everyone meets at least one person whom they would like to turn in as a prospect. It has to be used correctly. Lead the people to complete the cards immediately and return them to you. Ask for information on *one* prospect. Have you noticed that everyone knows one prospect? However, no one seems to know two.

The person filling out the card may not provide all of the information; however, he (or she) will sign the card. If we cannot find the prospect, we contact the person giving the information.

Another interesting thing about the "Who Do Card" is that you will get prospects of the same age of the people who give the information. For instance, if you need single-adult prospects, give the card to single adults. They know single adults. If you need high-school senior prospects, give the card to high-school seniors. They know high-school seniors. This card will give you prospects in the age group where you need them.

These are *instant prospects*. Use the card next Sunday and during the week you will have about all of the prospects you can use at one time.

You cannot buy the "Who Do Card." Make your own. Here is a sample.

| **WHO DO CARD** |
| --- |
| Who do you know that is a prospect for our Sunday School? |
| Name _____ |
| Address _____ |
| City _____ |
| Age _____   Grade _____ |
| Phone # _____ |
| Your Name _____ |

(2) Another method is called *People Search*. We suggest that when you take a People Search, do not try to survey your entire community (unless it is small). It is best to zone the community and take a People Search of one zone at a time. Continue to do this until you have worked out the entire field. You should have enough valid prospects to keep you visiting. The new prospects are up-to-date.

(3) In the last chapter we referred to the *Enrollment Kit*. The card used in the Kit has information for enrolling people on one side, but the back side of the Enrollment Card has a place for you to record the names of prospects.

For instance, we enroll Joe in the Sunday School. There is a good possibility that Joe will have several friends who are not enrolled. So, we ask, "Joe, now that you are enrolled, would you give me the names of two or three other people who are prospects? We want to visit them and try to enroll them." On the back of the Enrollment Card, there is a place to write their names. These cards can be used every week as a gleaning system to discover additional prospects.

*A prospect name is useless until it has been tabulated and assigned to the class that is responsible.* I suggest the "Reach Out Pocket and Card." This is an envelope and card. Once the information has been placed on the card, it should be given to the teacher or outreach leader of the class. That class is then responsible for reaching the prospect.

I don't believe in a prospect file (singular). I believe in prospect files (plural), a file for each teaching unit in the Sunday School. Later in this book, when we come to the outreach program, we will return to the use of this system.

(4) *Broadman Prospect Services* is a service of the Baptist Sunday School Board. If you are interested in this effective prospect discovery program, secure free information by calling 1/800/458-BSSB, or by asking about it in a Baptist Book Store.

(5) One of the largest groups of prospects in a church are the unenrolled church members. Each person should be enrolled in a class or department. Assign them to the class that is responsible.

## The Best Method for Enrolling Unenrolled Church Members

While examining this critical subject, let me share the most successful method we have used. First, make a list of the unenrolled church members. Second, tabulate these by age. Third, when possible, divide them into groups of thirty, fewer if needed, beginning with the oldest. Fourth, provide leadership, organization, and activity. Fifth, start *new* adult classes with the unenrolled church members, and almost every new class will thrive.

*Director of Prospecting*

The need for prospects is so valuable that at least one person should be elected to work solely with prospecting. In many churches the outreach director of the Sunday School is charged with all of the outreach activities, which includes prospecting. We find, however, that when a church earnestly determines to reach the community for Christ, it will have so many prospects that the outreach director cannot fulfill all of the activities or even keep up with them.

We suggest that you consider electing a director of prospecting. This person is charged with the responsibility of selecting the programs which are needed to discover prospects, tabulate, and place them in the hands of the responsible workers. At that point, the outreach director will secure and train the group leaders so the unreached are reached. Prospects are important. We will never reach our community for Christ until we have the information on every one of them.

Now it is time for you to complete this information on your Spiral. Place the number of prospects on the blank Spiral. In the next four blocks duplicate your enrollment goals. You may not be able to jump to the large number in one quarter, but reach as many as possible.

### CLARKSTON BAPTIST CHURCH
*Clarkston, GA*

| ITEM | OCT. '86 | OCT. '90 | INCREASE |
|------|----------|----------|----------|
| Enrollment | 970 | 1,244 | 277 |
| Prospects | 120 | 670 | 550 |
| Teaching Units | 42 | 55 | 13 |

| ITEM | OCT. '86 | OCT. '90 | INCREASE |
|---|---|---|---|
| Workers | 94 | 132 | 38 |
| Workers' Mtng. Att. | 0 | 42 | 42 |
| Training Awards | 30 | 60 | 30 |
| Weekly Contacts | 110 | 260 | 150 |
| Outreachers | 12 | 32 | 20 |
| SS Attendance | 370 | 503 | 133 |
| WS Attendance | 380 | 472 | 92 |
| Weekly Offerings | $6,800 | $10,072 | $3,272 |
| Baptisms | NA | NA | |

# The Church's Organizational Ministry

## *The Value of Teaching Units*

The organization is the skeleton of the church. Without it, the church would be unable to carry out the Great Commission. God is a God of organization. This is revealed in both the Old and New Testaments.

The Sunday School is the largest organization in the church, and every organization in the church grows when the Sunday School increases.

# 4

# The Value of Teaching Units

On the sample Spiral, as of October 1 we have two hundred enrolled, sixty-five prospects, and eight teaching units. Also, note the pluses and minuses. We have some strengths and some weaknesses.

In this chapter we will place our emphasis on *teaching units*. In the youth and adult areas, the teaching unit is usually called a "class," but in the children and preschool areas, the teaching unit is sometimes termed a "department." Therefore, the term *teaching unit* is used to refer to both class and department. A teaching unit is a group of pupils and a teacher.

Discover how many teaching units there are in your Sunday School. Place that number on the Spiral located in the back of this book. Shortly, we will evaluate to see if you have enough teaching units to care adequately for your membership.

My home is in Fort Myers, Florida, where we have lived for many years. We grow citrus fruit. Outside my door is a grapefruit tree. If the tree grows this year, it will produce grapefruit. It stands to reason, though, if the tree does not grow this year, there will be no grapefruit on the tree. The fruit develops on the *new* growth only. If you want a biblical illustration, study the grapevine. If the vine does not grow *this* year, there will be no grapes on it. The same basic principle works in the Sunday School. If we do not start new teaching units each year, there will be little or no growth. This is probably the most important growth item on the Spiral.

For instance, on the sample Spiral, we are considering the possibility of increasing the enrollment from 200 to 252 in one year. If we place fifty-two new people in the same eight teaching units there would be no growth. The teachers already have as much as they can do. As a result, even though the enrollment increases by fifty-two, the attendance probably will not increase. We must then create additional teaching units. The illustration of the grapefruit tree is extremely valuable to us. Most of the genuine and lasting growth is in new teaching units.

Here is the formula: 1/23/12. On an average one new teaching unit will increase the enrollment by twenty-three in twelve months, provided the unit is properly supported by the leadership.

Proper support is: (1) an adequate number of prospects; (2) an adequate place to meet; (3) an adequate worker staff; and (4) adequate encouragement.

If the new teaching unit is for adults, chances are the enrollment will increase more than twenty-three. If it is a youth, children's, or preschool unit it will be less than twenty-three.

The creation of new teaching units is imperative for Sunday School growth. There is some talk about changing the name of the classes or teaching units to "cells." Some churches are using "cell groups" and are experiencing outreach growth. *The secret of this growth is not in the name or location of the unit but the creation of new units. Growth comes about in new units, whether they are inside or outside the church building.*

If your goal is to increase the Sunday School enrollment by 230 the next year, you will need to start at least ten new teaching units, one new teaching unit for every twenty-three people you enroll.

If your enrollment increase goal is one-half of that, a 115 increase this year, you will need to create five new teaching units. It does not work any other way. Want a challenge? Create eleven new units each quarter, for a total of forty-four during the year and properly support them. Watch your enrollment grow by one-thousand and your attendance increase about four hundred. The offerings and baptisms will grow in proportion.

Some churches have gone to a master-teaching program or a large-class concept. After studying church growth since I was a teenager, I believe the best approach is to concentrate on the small-class concept.

Let me explain why. At a major college or university in your state, there is a possibility you may find three, four or five hundred students in one class. It may be the finest educational institution in your state, even with five hundred enrolled in one class. How can we justify the small-class concept by saying, "We can't teach if we have more than twenty-five"?

The Sunday School is not merely a teaching organization. It is also *a ministering organization.* How can we minister to the people enrolled in our Sunday School and reach all of the prospects if this is not done through the small teaching unit? Obviously, we have no other organization or method to do this. Small Sunday School classes give us an opportunity to minister. Here is an actual illustration. One Saturday night the telephone rang. A lady who was a widow with one son was shocked when she answered. The sheriff's department called to report, "Mrs. Smith, your teenage son was picked up tonight on a marijuana charge." She and her son, Christian people, attended church every week. She could not understand this and was totally crushed. She did not know what to do. Officials would not allow her to visit her son that Saturday night, but the next morning she went to Sunday School. If there had been fifty, seventy-five, or one hundred people in the classroom, would she have been able to share her burden with all of those people? No. But, instead, her class had twenty-four people enrolled, and there were ten to twelve people in the class that morning.

In that small unit, they ministered to one another and cared for one another. They prayed together. She was able to share her hurt with her classmates, and their encouragement carried her through.

*Ministry is the key to Sunday School.* We need to concentrate on the small-teaching-unit concept. Earlier we looked at the sample Spiral and saw that there are eight teaching units. Let us evaluate.

Divide 8, the number of teaching units, into the enrollment of 200. The result is one teaching unit, on an average, for every twenty-five people enrolled in the Sunday School. Obviously, some of the teaching units are larger.

The classes, on an average, are too large. As recorded in an earlier chapter, the best ratio is an average of one teaching unit for every twelve to eighteen people enrolled in the Sunday School. That is an average for the *whole* Sunday School. At this size they are large enough to be healthy, yet small enough to grow. There needs to be a separate Spiral for each teaching unit in the Sunday School because the enrollment and worker ratios vary considerably. Information about this can be found in the last four chapters.

*Now, evaluate your school.* The Spiral provides a projection. Divide 18 (we recommend twelve to eighteen enrolled in the average teaching unit) into the projected Sunday School enrollment of 252. The result is 14. During the year, we need to increase the teaching units from eight to fourteen.

*We find that when an adult class reaches twelve months of age, it ceases to grow.* After this it may grow a little, but under normal circumstances it reaches its maturity in a year. If you want to reach additional single adults, and your classes have celebrated their first birthday, you must start another.

Do you need to start an international class? The Spiral churches discover that when they start a class, it reaches its maximum enrollment in about thirty days. People will become involved when we show an interest in their welfare. Concentrate on the international people who live in your community.

What about an additional class for senior adults? Or a class for median adults? Or a class for young adults? If your present classes are a year old, create at least one more in each of these areas.

What about an additional youth class? Are your present classes over one year of age? Start one more youth class.

What about a new children's department? We cannot overlook this group. Jesus took them in His arms and blessed them. Ours is an equal responsibility. What about starting some additional preschool departments? Churches with all of the preschool departments they need grow much faster than churches with mediocre accommodations.

Consider a pastor's class. If you need information about this, call 1/800/458-BSSB and ask about a videotape, "The Pastor's Class," which explains it.

You also need to consider an Adults Away department. How

many of our adults are in the military service? Others work in businesses which move them around the nation and world. We need to have a class to minister to their needs.

And what about a Homebound Department? One church had difficulty lining up enough workers to teach the lesson, a most important part of the Homebound Ministry. So, they installed a conference telephone hookup with ten phones on the system!

On Sunday morning one of the Homebound members telephoned nine other Homebound members, and the minister of education taught them the Sunday School lesson via phone. The church provided every member of the Homebound minister a large-print adult quarterly. That was not the end of it. When those nine people hung up, the telephoner called nine others. When they completed their lesson, she called nine more. In approximately one hour the minister of education taught twenty-seven people with a conference telephone hookup. During the week, visitors from the church visited in the homes of the Homebound but did not need to teach the lesson.

Someone may ask, "Can we count them?" Yes, we can. At least they are awake. We need to color outside of the lines. We will never get the job done with traditional thinking. We live in an electronic age. Why not involve electronics in the teaching of the Bible?

What about a class for the mentally handicapped? When I accepted my last pastorate, we had a small class of handicapped people. When I left nineteen years later, we had one of the largest classes for the mentally handicapped in our entire Southern Baptist Convention. There is a need in almost every community.

What about a class for the deaf? Often they have no place to study the Bible. Consider this type of class. How about a Cradle Roll department? I think I was enrolled in Cradle Roll before I was born. We need Cradle Roll. We are in a baby boom. Look around—you will find your prospects. Enroll these preschoolers. We must minister to the parents before the child is born, as well as after.

You are already at capacity attendance? I encourage you to start a *second* Sunday School. *Take at least nine months to develop it.* Let your members know when and how you are going to do it, who will be involved, and other details that enter into developing a second school. This is imperative. Most churches can have a second Sunday School. Some may even consider three.

What about having Sunday School at some other time during the week? For instance, why not have Sunday School on Sunday night preceding the worship service? Some might ask, "Won't that interfere with other programs?" No, because we will involve a group of people who could not attend on Sunday morning. You already have the preaching service, so plan a graded Sunday School to go along with it.

Look at the possibility of starting a Sunday School on Wednesday night. There is no reason why we can't use Wednesday night as a time for a graded Sunday School program. In fact, I hope the day will come when we will have a graded Sunday School every night in the week. With the large number of unreached people in our nation today, we cannot build enough buildings. We ought to fill our buildings with Bible study classes every night of the week. Let the pastor preach his sermon every night during the week—and when he preaches it on Sunday morning, he will have it "down pat"!

Here is the bottom line. Too many of our Sunday Schools are organized for maintenance; that is, they are organized only to care for the people who are enrolled. But we need to organize for growth. The only way this can be accomplished is to increase the number of teaching units. Survey your community. Discover all of your prospects. Tabulate them by age or by school grade. Organize to reach everyone, and then go after them.

My last thought in this chapter is the one I started with: One new teaching unit will produce twenty-three new enrollees in twelve months when properly supported. May God help us to start thousands of teaching units to reach millions of people.

Before we leave this chapter you need to complete the Teaching Units column on your Spiral. Divide 18 into the projected Sunday School enrollment. This reveals the number of units required at the end of the year. Place this number at the end of the column and determine how many you need in each quarter.

**FIRST BAPTIST CHURCH**
*Tuscaloosa, AL*

| ITEM | JAN. '82 | MAR. '90 | INCREASE |
|---|---|---|---|
| Enrollment | 1,750 | 3,561 | 1,811 |
| Prospects | 400 | 1,575 | 1,175 |
| Teaching Units | 55 | 119 | 64 |
| Workers | 220 | 446 | 226 |
| Workers' Mtng. Att. | 40 | 65 | 15 |
| Training Awards | 50 | 50 | 0 |
| Weekly Contacts | 200 | 544 | 344 |
| Outreachers | 50 | 61 | 11 |
| SS Attendance | 900 | 1,471 | 571 |
| WS Attendance | 1,300 | 1,725 | 425 |
| Weekly Offering | $13,870 | $28,461 | $14,591 |
| Baptisms | 48 | NA | NA |

# The Church's Discipleship Ministry

*The Value of Workers*
*The Value of the Workers' Planning Meeting*
*The Value of Training*

On-the-job training is one of the best discipleship programs of the church. A new Christian should be enlisted to accept a position of leadership as a starting point. Meeting with other Sunday School workers each week helps the new Christian grow. A study of Christian doctrine could be the first in a study plan for discipleship.

# 5

# The Value of Workers

We have studied enrollment, prospects and teaching units. Now we focus our attention on workers. It is rare to find a church with a sufficiency. One of the most effective parts of the Spiral is found in this chapter: how to have all of the workers you need and have them trained before beginning their work.

The Spiral is an evaluation tool. On the sample Spiral notice that we have eighteen workers in the Sunday School. That is an average of one worker per eleven people enrolled in Sunday School.

In the evaluation there is a minus because there are not enough workers. There should be at least one worker for every five people enrolled in Sunday School in order to adequately minister to their needs.

The result shows that we need fifty workers by the end of the year. With eighteen workers in place, subtract 18 from 50 and discover that we need to enlist and involve thirty-two additional workers by the end of the year. Divide 32 by 4 (quarters) and we learn that we need an additional eight workers each quarter. By following this plan we can add thirty-two workers to the existing eighteen to produce the needed fifty by the end of the year.

Since it is easier to add additional workers each quarter than trying to enlist all of the workers at one time, the Spiral becomes a valuable goal-setting tool. At a glance it reveals whether we need workers and, if so, how many.

I have made several hundred surveys on the effect of workers on the Sunday School attendance. Here is the result of one. Church A has 190 enrolled in Sunday School and church B has 188. Church A has ten workers or one worker for nineteen enrollees. Church B has thirty-six workers or one worker for five enrollees.

The Sunday School attendance in church A is sixty, or 32 percent of the enrollment; in church B the average attendance is 120, or 64 percent of the enrollment. The primary difference in the two churches is the worker ratio. The number of training awards are about the same in each church. The larger number of workers produced a larger number of outreachers and contacts, which resulted in more involvement by the members.

The following chart is the result of about 250 surveys:

| RATIO OF WORKERS | PERCENT OF ENROLLMENT IN ATTENDANCE |
|---|---|
| 1 to 5-7 | 58 percent in attendance |
| 1 to 8, 9 | 43 percent in attendance |
| 1 to 10 up | 36 percent in attendance |

Here is a list of the people counted as workers in this ratio.

1. Sunday School teachers
2. Class outreach leaders
3. Department directors
4. Department outreach leaders
5. Division directors
6. Division outreach leaders
7. Pastor
8. Other staff members
9. Minister of Education
10. Sunday School director
11. Outreach director
12. Adult group (care) leaders
13. Bus ministry workers

Other workers in the Sunday School are pivotal, but, in this ratio, we counted only those listed.

Before continuing, add the workers in your Sunday School and place that number on the blank Spiral in the back of this book. Divide the number of workers into your enrollment to discover the ratio of workers to enrollment. Check the formula to see where you are in the percentage of attendance.

*Enlist and Train Potential Workers*

Here is the most successful program we use in the Spiral churches, the most effective method I have used in the forty-five years of my involvement as a church leader.

*Conducting Potential Sunday School Worker Training* is the book we use. You may obtain it by calling 1-800/458-BSSB, by computer from E.C.O.S. (Easy Church Order System), CIS, 127 Ninth Ave., Nashville, TN 37234, or from your area Christian bookstore.

Conduct four potential Sunday School workers' training sessions a year. Traditionally, we train Sunday School workers during Preparation Week. We enlist workers, train, and put them to work once a year. This has not produced enough workers. I encourage you to provide four training classes each year.

Look at the sample Spiral and note the projected number of workers you will need each quarter. Look again to see how this number is determined.

With eighteen workers now, at the end of the first quarter, you will need twenty-six workers—a net gain of eight workers. In a Sunday School of this size, you will probably lose an average of two workers per quarter. With the need for a net gain of eight, plus the probability of replacing the two whom we lose, we must enlist ten additional workers during the quarter. Use this method to determine the additional number of workers each quarter. It is imperative to select the best teacher for the *Conducting Potential Sunday School Worker Training* class. You may say, "That person is already teaching in Sunday School."

I hope so, but that person's influence will never go much beyond the small group of people in the class. You should utilize that teacher to train all of your future workers. Good potential workers will not sit at the feet of a bad teacher. You must have the best.

If you do not have the proper teacher in your membership, you may want to consider purchasing a series of videotapes using the same material that is in the textbook. The teachers on these videos are some of the best in the nation. Call 1-800/458-BSSB for information about the videotapes entitled *Training Potential Sunday School Workers.*

On the first Sunday of each quarter do two things:

1. *Pray for new workers.* Encourage the church members to kneel at the front of your church and pray specifically for ten new workers. Don't pray for *more* workers or *additional* workers. Pray specifically for the number you need. That is what the Lord instructed us to do. "Pray ye therefore the Lord of the harvest, that he will send forth laborers..." (Matt. 9:38). Before the members get off their knees, encourage them to pray one more prayer: "Lord, am I one of the workers?" Do this on the first Sunday of every quarter.

2. *Enlist the new workers.* Elaine is the best teacher we have. "Elaine, we want you, now that you are no longer teaching the other class, to be responsible, under the leadership of the Holy Spirit, to find the ten people whom the Lord has called out."

Does Elaine have a hard job? No. She has one of the easiest. Why? The same Holy Spirit who called out these potential workers in answer to prayer is now leading Elaine to find them. She will discover them. In fact, we are discovering that people will volunteer because they know the Lord has spoken to them concerning this matter.

*When the workers are enlisted, they should be told they are under no obligation to accept a role in the Sunday School when they complete the training.* If they desire to return to their Sunday School classes, without working as a teacher, outreach leader, secretary, etc., they will be better Christians because they have explored the will of God for their lives. This also gives them the choice of studying the possibilities without the pressure. Potential workers will complete this class and go to work.

Elaine, beginning the first Sunday of the quarter, finds these potential workers, and enlists them for the leader-training class. She has five weeks in which to do this.

On the sixth Sunday of each quarter, Elaine begins teaching the potential workers using the book, *Training Potential Sunday School Workers.*

She has studied the book and found three agendas. We have discovered that the second agenda is the best. For instance, the first agenda is scheduled for sixteen weeks. Churches using this discover that about 50 percent of those who start the class drop out. It seems that the program is too long. Also, when the sixteen-week program is used with the Spiral (a thirteen-week segment) we have a calendar conflict because a quarter is only thirteen weeks in length. The class overlaps into the next quarter. Elaine decides to use the "Fast Track, Sequence B" because it is eight weeks in length. We have discovered that 80 to 90 percent of those who start this agenda complete it and go to work in the Sunday School.

Another strong part of this class is that it meets Sunday morning during Sunday School, Sunday evening, and on Wednesday night, either before or following the midweek prayer service. Elaine will train the people while they are already at the church.

Sunday morning, Sunday night, and Wednesday night—three hours of training each week multiplied by eight weeks—means that every potential worker will receive twenty-four hours of training before they go to work. That will revolutionize the Sunday School. We are discovering that the quality of workers who come out of this course is so impressive that in many churches some of the present workers are asking for a leave of absence in order take the course.

This is only the beginning. Let me show you more about the Fast Track, Sequence B. There are five practical units of study. For instance, on the second Sunday morning, Elaine takes her ten potential workers and visits a preschool and a children's department. Then, in their session on Sunday night, they discuss what they observed. This is a good time to invite teachers and leaders from these age groups to share with the potential workers. The next Sunday morning, Elaine and her class observe youth and adult classes. When they assemble on Sunday night they discuss what they experienced. Youth and adult workers should be invited to participate in the Sunday evening sessions.

Potential workers are exposed to the available areas of service. Elaine is helping these ten people discover where God wants them to serve. It helps the potential worker to understand the needs, opportunities, and some of the responsibilities in each age group. When they know this it is easier for them to discover God's will for their lives.

In the course, *Training Potential Sunday School Workers,* there is a session on the workers' meeting: What happens in a workers' meeting, who attends, how long is it, when does it meet, etc?

Another session is on the weekly outreach program. What night? Who talks? Who is to be visited? The potential workers will know what is expected of them when they become workers. You may think, *That is an aggressive program. People will not get that involved.*

Let me share some of the statistics we have gathered. From 80 to 90 percent of the people who enroll in this course will graduate and actually go to work in the Sunday Schools. This is one of the most effective training methods for potential workers we have used. Why does it work so well?

1.  The people are prayed for.
2.  They are enlisted one at a time.
3.  They are trained for specific jobs.
4.  They are placed in positions where God has called them.

New workers are more effective and lasting when their enlistment and training are done correctly.

This is the plan Jesus used when He selected His apostles.

1.  He prayed all night before enlisting them.
2.  He enlisted them one at a time.
3.  He trained them.
4.  He placed them in the proper place of responsibility.

Where does Elaine receive the help she needs to teach this class adequately? The textbook she uses tells her what to do before, during, and following the session. All of the resource material is in the book.

The people who graduate receive twenty-four hours (three hours a week times eight weeks) of practical training. They also receive credit for three of the six study course books required for the

Leadership Diploma. Two of the texts they study during the class are general books about Sunday School work. The third course relates to the age group in which the student has decided to work. This is one of the most potent training sessions used in our churches today.

Look in the media center at your church. You may already have this book. In four hundred churches that use this method of enlisting, training and placing potential workers, the number of workers increased by more than ten thousand. After discounting the number of workers who quit for some reason, there was a net increase of over ten thousand workers! Most of these were graduates of the potential leader training class.

On the thirteenth week of the quarter, the last Sunday of the quarter, the church graduates Elaine's class. The new workers will be placed in the Sunday School organization where their gifts are needed. Some may be asked to create new teaching units.

Let me encourage you to make another step. When you conclude this twenty-four-hour period of training, have a graduation service. Have someone play "Pomp and Circumstance." Borrow caps and gowns. Let the people graduate. This will honor the students and encourage others to become involved in this training program.

1.  The number of NEW teaching units determines the enrollment growth.
2.  The ratio of workers to enrollment determines the attendance.

I am not aware of two more important Sunday Schools principles than these. Enlist and train as many workers as you can. Utilize their gifts for the Lord and for the people of your community.

### SEQUOYAH HILLS BAPTIST CHURCH
Tulsa, OK

| ITEMS | FEB. '83 | OCT. '90 | INCREASE |
|---|---|---|---|
| Enrollment | 1,219 | 2,117 | 898 |
| Prospects | 630 | 1,950 | 1,320 |
| Teaching Units | 61 | 98 | 34 |
| Workers | 138 | 267 | 129 |

| ITEMS | FEB. '83 | OCT. '90 | INCREASE |
|---|---|---|---|
| Workers' Mtng. Att. | 80 | 135 | 55 |
| Training Awards | 55 | 160 | 105 |
| Weekly Contacts | 485 | 950 | 475 |
| Outreachers | 42 | 95 | 53 |
| SS Attendance | 495 | 618 | 123 |
| WS Attendance | 490 | 610 | 120 |
| Weekly Offerings | $7,100 | $9,500 | $2,400 |
| Baptisms | 64 | 157 | 93 |

# 6

# The Value of the Workers' Planning Meeting

In this chapter we will examine the workers' planning meeting. Some refer to this meeting as the weekly workers' meeting, and others call it the officers and teachers' meeting.

On the sample Spiral there are six people in attendance. This is a minus because there are not enough of the workers present for planning. We need to have at least 75 percent of the workers present. The reason the percentage is so high is because this is a planning meeting. It is difficult to plan if at least three-fourths of the workers are not in attendance.

We can establish each quarter's goal for the rest of the year. Three-fourths of the twenty-six workers we have next quarter is a goal of at least nineteen. For the second quarter, twenty-five workers in attendance, then thirty-two, and in the final quarter, thirty-eight workers in attendance. The Spiral keeps us abreast of what is going on. If the workers' meetings are not functioning as they should, we can adjust them.

I believe this is the most important meeting in a church. This is not to indicate that we must choose between a worship service or a Sunday School and a workers' meeting. I recall in the early days of my pastorates I did not use the workers' meeting as it was designed. As a result, it felt like the burden of the whole church lay on my shoulders. The load was too heavy, even for a young man. I became discouraged even to the point where I considered resigning and leaving my sacred calling. But I learned to use the workers' meeting. From that day on, my pastorate became far more successful, and I had some relief from the great responsibility. Every Wednesday night, I brought the workers together, planned with them, motivated them, let them know I loved and needed them, and helped them make plans for the following weeks. The workers came together weekly and received what I could give them, what they could gain from each other and from the materials. This produced motivation, and the educational program assumed a new vitality.

The Sunday School workers were the best visitors in the church, our most motivated people. So, instead of me doing all the work by myself, there was an army of people helping to minister.

Pastors, assemble your workers together on Wednesday night or whenever you can. Meet with them and share your vision. Let them know how much you depend on them. Offer them your support and encouragement. You will discover a new day in your church.

### Continuing Motivation

Some of us like to camp in the open air. Isn't it peculiar that, even in the heat of summer, perhaps the first thing we do is build a camp fire? Let us assume we have several sticks of wood. Once the fire is started, we place the wood on it. As long as the pieces of wood are together there is light, life, warmth, and energy. When we separate them, they become black charcoal, without light, life, heat, or energy. The secret is in their remaining together.

The main people in the church concerned about the Bible study ministry are those who work in the Sunday School. When there is no weekly workers' meeting, they are separate entities without motivation, light, life, warmth, or energy. By assembling weekly—molding their prayer, interest, and concern—then light, life, warmth, and energy are created.

This is the best method I know for developing a *continuing motivation*. When there is no weekly meeting, there is little stimulus. A properly conducted weekly meeting produces inspiration.

Here are twelve reasons why I feel we need a weekly workers' meeting:

1. *Fellowship is developed in the workers' meeting.* People are often so busy they do not know who is working in the Sunday School. The workers should join together for fellowship. This is a part of deepening their commitment to the Lord, to the church and to one another.

2. *Better leaders are developed in the workers' meeting.* This is the place where better leaders are developed. We use materials to help them improve their relationship with God, do a better job in teaching and ministering, and grow spiritually.

3. *Team spirit is developed in weekly workers' meetings.* There needs to be a team spirit. I live in Florida. Can you imagine the coach of the Miami Dolphins allowing his players to omit practice all week and then, an hour before the game, bringing them together for a little pep talk and sending them onto the field to win? No way. The players come together to plan, study and practice. There is a team spirit, a oneness. Could it be we are not growing great Sunday Schools and churches because our workers have no team spirit? Esprit de corps needs to be created.

4. *Commitment is developed in workers' meetings.* What about commitment? Where will the commitment of our Sunday School workers come from if we don't have this meeting? Not in the Sunday morning, Sunday evening or Wednesday night service. Share with the workers what their responsibilities are so they can be committed to them. The weekly workers' meeting is the place to accomplish this.

5. *Prayer life is developed in the workers' meeting.* Prayer time is valuable in the workers meeting. Many Sunday School members have never been prayed for by name. If we did nothing else in the weekly workers' meeting but to pray for each Sunday School member and prospect by name, it would change the spirit of the educational program of the church.

6. *Ministry is developed in the workers' meeting.* What about ministry? One of the major responsibilities of the Sunday School is to minister to the needs of the people. Workers often hurt more

than the people to whom they minister. A time is essential when the leaders of the Sunday School can *minister to those who minister.* That can happen during the workers' meeting.

7. *Preparation takes place in workers' meetings.* Where do we prepare for next Sunday, for the next unit, for the next quarter? Obviously, some of this is done at home, but some can be carried out only in the classrooms. Class and department rooms need to be cleaned and arranged for next Sunday. Workers need to plan for the activities.

8. *Promotion takes place in workers' meetings.* Where do we promote whatever we promote if we do not have a planning meeting?

9. *Outreach is planned and promoted in the workers' meeting.* Where do we plan, promote and report on the outreach program if we do not have this meeting?

10. *Correlation of work takes place in the workers' meeting.* Where do we correlate, dovetail, the work of the Sunday School if we do not spend some time making it happen?

11. *Evaluation takes place during workers' meetings.* Where do we evaluate our effectiveness without this meeting? We must know where we *were,* where we *are,* and where *we are going.*

12. *Growth takes place as a result of workers' meetings.* Without these meaningful sessions, it is almost impossible to grow a church. Here the incentive is placed in the hearts and lives of the workers, and a commitment is secured from those workers to reach, evangelize, and disciple the community (as well as the world).

Some churches have difficulty in building attendance at their workers' meeting because: (1) In many cases the leadership does not know what to do in the workers' meeting. (2) Some of our meetings are ineffective because the workers have no idea what to do when they attend the sessions.

A monthly magazine which should be provided to all age-group workers in large Sunday Schools is *The Sunday School Leader:*

*Larger Church Edition.* It contains motivational articles and guidelines to correctly conduct the workers' meeting, and tells the leaders what to do prior to, during, and following the meeting. If you are in a small church, do not feel left out. Also available, but quarterly, is *The Sunday School Leader: Smaller Church Edition.*

The magazine also furnishes helpful information for workers who leave the general session of the workers' meeting and go into the age-group meetings.

Sunday School workers can be divided into three categories: 1. Administrators; 2. Educators; and 3. Outreachers.

The term "weekly workers' meeting" seems to be better than "officers and teachers' meeting." "Officers and teachers' meeting" normally indicates that the only people who attend are administrators and educators. The officers are the *administrators*. The teachers are the *educators*. The outreach director, outreach leaders and group leaders are the *outreachers*. The meeting should include more than just the officers and teachers. Workers' meeting includes all of the workers—the administrators, the educators, and the outreachers.

One of the most effective schedules for the weekly workers' meeting is as follows. This is used in some of the churches that are involved in the Advanced Spiral. It needs to be customized by every church:

*General Session    10-15 minutes*

Begin with a general session. Every worker in the Sunday School is encouraged to attend the general meeting. The pastor, minister of education, Sunday School director or general outreach director normally leads this session. The pastor should take about three to five minutes of this time to motivate and encourage. After the general meeting, traditionally, the officers and teachers go to their class and department rooms to prepare for the next week's activities.

*Division or Department Time   10-15 minutes*

If you have departments or divisions (usually found in larger Sunday Schools), there needs to be some time in these for planning.

*Specific Planning Time   30-45 minutes*

1. Administrators and Educators—Workers go to their rooms to set up, clean up, prepare for the future sessions and pray.
2. Outreachers—All outreach workers (outreach directors, outreach leaders and group leaders) should gather together weekly, during this time, to prepare the outreach program for the week. Planning in this area has been neglected in most of our churches. Very few churches schedule a time to PREPARE for outreach. Subjects for this meeting should be:
   —type of outreach
   —time of outreach
   —persons in outreach
   —subjects of outreach
   —training for outreach

An excellent study with which to begin this session is to study *Training Outreach Leaders in Sunday School.*

*Closing   5 minutes*

The administrators, educators, and outreachers should meet together for about five minutes to encourage and inform about what each group is doing for next week. Place the average attendance of your workers' meeting on your Spiral. Complete the numbers for the entire year. Then evaluate your meeting.

**MEMORIAL BAPTIST CHURCH**
*Grapevine, TX*

| ITEM | OCT. '87 | OCT. '90 | INCREASE |
|------|---------|---------|---------|
| Enrollment | 663 | 1,086 | 423 |
| Prospects | 204 | 896 | 692 |
| Teaching Units | 23 | 48 | 25 |
| Workers | 51 | 126 | 75 |
| Workers' Mtng. Att. | 13 | 65 | 52 |

| ITEM | OCT. '87 | OCT. '90 | INCREASE |
|---|---|---|---|
| Training Awards | 0 | 39 | 39 |
| Weekly Contacts | 115 | 486 | 353 |
| Outreachers | 11 | 47 | 36 |
| SS Attendance | 262 | 492 | 230 |
| WS Attendance | 283 | 540 | 257 |
| Weekly Offering | $6,050 | $9,200 | $3,150 |
| Baptisms | 12 | 70 | 58 |

# 7

# The Value of Training

We ought to emblazon on the walls of our churches and our desks this motto: WE CANNOT GROW CHURCHES WITH UNTRAINED LEADERSHIP. We have never done it. We will never do it. Leadership must be trained if we reach people, teach them, and minister to their needs.

As we study the sample Spiral, we discover that during the last quarter there were only two training awards. These are quarter blocks, thirteen-week blocks. The goal that we set for training awards needs to equal one-half the number of workers each quarter. Since there are eighteen workers, we needed at least nine training awards (study courses completed) during that quarter.

During the next quarter, with twenty-six workers, the goal is thirteen training awards. The quarter in which we have thirty-four workers, we need seventeen awards and with forty-two workers, twenty-one training awards. In the final quarter with fifty workers, the goal is twenty-five awards. This gives us a quarterly report on how much training is being done. If we do not set goals, we will not reach them.

Every Sunday School needs a person in charge of training—the director of Teaching Improvement and Training. When I entered college, the registrar helped me design the courses of study for each year. These courses were designed so that, by the time I completed my college education, I would receive a diploma. The same process followed in seminary.

We need to have a designed program of training in our Sunday Schools and churches. The director of Teaching Improvement and Training should plan with every Sunday School worker. A program should be designed to offer specific courses of study for each quarter during the first year, the second year, and so on, until each worker has completed the courses needed to receive the Leadership and Advanced Leadership diplomas. Other leadership diplomas are available to fulfill the training needs.

The director of Teaching Improvement and Training needs to be sure that every Sunday School worker, plus potential workers, has a Church Study Course number. This places each person on the computer at the Baptist Sunday School Board so that every time a study course is completed and Form 725 is turned in it is recorded to the person's record of training.

Periodically, the Sunday School Board sends out a transcript which informs those who are enrolled which courses they have completed and which courses they need to complete to receive a certain diploma.

A third action the director of Teaching Improvement and Training should do is to plan and promote a study course for each quarter of the year. At least four courses should be offered. There are several ways people can receive credit for their study:

*Individual Study*

The student can secure the book, read it, answer the questions at the end of each chapter, and fulfill the requirements for receiving credit.

*Large-Group Study*

The church should provide several large-group studies. One could be a January Bible Study. There was a time when our churches packed the buildings with people studying the books of the Bible. Some pastors decided that, instead of teaching the book in one week, they would preach on it every Sunday night or teach it every Wednesday night for several weeks. I feel we should concentrate this study into a one-week period.

*Retreats*

Some churches could enhance their studies with retreats. For instance, on Saturday morning prepare breakfast for all who attend. Study until lunch. Bring a sack lunch or prepare a noon meal. Continue to study after lunch until the course is completed. What an exciting way to motivate the people!

*Age-Group Studies*

There is a need for some age-group studies. For instance, assemble the preschool workers. Invite a preschool specialist to train them. Do the same with the children, youth, and adult workers and general officers. This is an excellent method of unifying the workers in a group.

*Associational Study*

The Association is constantly promoting studies. State or approved leaders conduct these meetings. ASSIST (Associational Sunday School Improvement Support Team) members, in some cases, are used to lead the training, providing again another opportunity for training.

*Conference Center Study*

Most states have Convention-wide training. In addition, there are two major conference centers where the leaders can be trained.

*Graduation*

Following a training course, have a graduation, a celebration. Let the people understand that this is a momentous occasion in our lives. Most churches have a *Church Study Course Catalog.* Hundreds of study course books are listed under various headings in that publication. The workers can see what they need to study in order to receive available diplomas.

I do not preach something that I have not practiced. At the time of this writing I have completed every study course book the Baptist Sunday School Board has published, with the exception of some specialized and language books. This is not shared with you to boast, but because I believe it is one of the finest training series available.

Contact a local Baptist Book Store in order to secure a copy of this catalog. Church leaders of all denominations can benefit from these courses. Go back to a statement made in the beginning of this chapter. We will never grow churches with untrained leaders. They must be trained.

Before we leave this chapter, add the number of training awards you had in the last quarter. Place this number on your Spiral and make your evaluation.

### WALNUT STREET BAPTIST CHURCH
*Jonesboro, AR*

| ITEM | JAN. '83 | MAR. '90 | INCREASE |
|------|---------|----------|----------|
| Enrollment | 445 | 877 | 432 |
| Prospects | 50 | 500 | 450 |
| Teaching units | 28 | 49 | 21 |
| Workers | 49 | 90 | 41 |
| Workers' Mtng. Att. | 0 | 40 | 40 |
| Training Awards | 0 | 150 | 150 |
| Weekly Contacts | 50 | 300 | 250 |
| Outreachers | 0 | 60 | 60 |
| SS Attendance | 245 | 400 | 155 |
| WS Attendance | 286 | 425 | 139 |
| Weekly Offerings | $4,200 | $5,500 | $1,300 |
| Baptisms | 16 | 37 | 21 |

# The Church's Building Program

## The Value of Space

The largest organization in the church is the Sunday School. Its needs are considered first when additional educational space is constructed.

# 8
# The Value of Space

Following a "space walk," I discover that we have twelve spaces where classes can meet. Since eight of them are used now, only four are empty.

On the sample Spiral, there is a plus because there are some available spaces. Below this block are the numbers 11, 12, 13, and 14. This is because, in the next four quarters, we will need that many spaces to house the total teaching units.

By the end of the third quarter the church will need thirteen spaces, so we will be out of space. In the third quarter there is an asterisk (*) which shows that by July 1, there will be no places in the building to expand. Additional space will be needed. This is vital information for long-range planning.

Churches that have been growing rapidly in the Advance Spiral program have become innovative in discovering additional space. Here are some of the places where they have found additional temporary space:

1. *Claim the available space.* Walk through the educational building. You may discover bales of hay, cradles, dolls, angel wings, and tables and chairs with broken legs. We rarely repair broken furniture—we simply store it. It is possible to find about 15 percent more available space if we clean up. The system we use is called "The Pick-up Truck." The system is used at night at the back door of the church by people who keep information to themselves. Again, I write this with tongue in cheek.

2. *Adjust the space.* Draw a floor plan of your educational building. There is no value in drawing it to scale. Merely draw in the walls where they are. Now, place four items of information in each room.

1. What age group meets in the room.
2. The square feet in the room.
3. The enrollment of the class which meets in the room.
4. The average attendance of the class.

This information enables you to determine which teaching units have room to grow and which have reached their capacity. Place the larger classes in the larger rooms and the smaller ones in the smaller rooms. There will be some classes you cannot move from one space to another. For instance, you need to keep the young adults in close proximity to the preschoolers. Do not place preschoolers above or below the ground level.

You may also discover there are some classes you dare not move. The members bought the carpet for the floor and put drapes on the windows. They may have a brass plaque by the door with names on it. Make the needed adjustments. There is one caution: never place a growing class in a small room. Give it a chance to grow.

Once we adjust the classes to fit the rooms, we are finding about 15 percent more space. There is a possibility you could discover 30 percent additional space with these first two adjustments.

3. *Use round tables.* Sell or give away the rectangular-shaped tables in the church. It seems we purchase these so we can fellowship around them, but think about it. You can't fellowship very well around a rectangular-shaped table. About the only person you can talk with is the person sitting directly in front of you. To be polite to the person who is sitting next to you, you must make a 90-degree turn. Rectangular tables hinder fellowship. Instead, I suggest that you purchase five-foot round tables. This is the best furniture to utilize space I have seen in more than forty-five years of church work.

Here are some benefits:

1. Only about eight or nine people can sit around a five-foot round table. Therefore, you will never have a Sunday School class which is too large. When the table gets full, secure another table.

2. Some of the teachers, who have been standing and lecturing to their classes, will need to sit down and teach. If the teacher uses visuals, they can be placed in the center of the table where everyone can examine them simultaneously.

3. The most important benefit is that they provide a better use of space. Most of our churches have several large rooms. We have cafeterias, auditoriums, gymnasiums, department assembly rooms, and other large rooms which we cannot use except for one purpose.

You can take any large room, fill it with round tables, and utilize every inch of it with adult and older youth classes. No class will disturb another, because when people sit around a round table they talk with one another. Of course, this is not the ideal condition, but it provides space for classes when you have none. Some churches can double the number of teaching units by purchasing round tables. There is no need to construct partitions to place between them.

4. *Look for adjacent space.*

A. Walk about one-half mile down each street leading from your church. Probably you will discover several kinds of buildings. Ask a question about each structure: "Can this building be used for Sunday School space?" For instance, some of your church members live within that half-mile radius and would love to have an adult class meet in their living room on Sunday. All you need to do is ask. Each room provides space for an additional teaching unit with twenty to twenty-five enrolled and ten to fifteen in attendance. The space costs nothing.

B. There may be a Seventh-day Adventist Church in the area. They do not use their buildings on Sundays. In some communities they are lending their buildings.

C. There may be a bank building close by. What about the possibility of using a conference room for an adult class?

D. One church is using part of a funeral home. They do not have funerals on Sunday morning, and, when asked, the funeral director welcomed them. The minister of education placed an adult men's class in that funeral home. They named that class, "The Lazarus Class." The minister of education quipped, "If you have a class that is dead or dying, place them in a funeral home. They will look around, see the caskets, and they will come to life faster than Lazarus."

E. What about a school? One of the churches I pastored leased an elementary school located about one-half block from the church. On Sunday morning we placed all of the first through sixth graders in the school. The furniture fit the children. We took the space they had been using and developed it into adult educational space. Can you imagine the gigantic leap we had in Sunday School attendance from the very first day we entered the redesigned building? As soon as possible a new children's building was constructed, and the children returned.

5. *Construct additional space.* Sooner or later you will need to build additional space. Contact your state Sunday School director. If he does not have the architectural responsibility in your state, he will give you the name of the person who can help you. That person can lead you through the entire process at no cost, and it will save a bundle of money.

I close this chapter by calling your attention to this equation. Place your information in the blanks.

TOTAL SQUARE FEET divided by 40 sq = MSSA _____
(Maximum Sunday School Attendance)

Subtract 20% _____
(Actual Sunday School Attendance) = ASSA _____

First, discover the total square feet of educational space. Use a tape measure and do an outside building measurement.

If you use part of the worship center for educational space, count the part which you use. Divide the total square feet of educational space by 40 square feet which includes all of the support area—restrooms, maintenance rooms, stairs, halls, etc. You will need 40-45 square feet per attendant. We are using 40 square feet in this illustration. The total square feet divided by 40 will give you the MSSA (Maximum Sunday School Attendance). That is the maximum number of people you can place in your educational space. Subtract 20 percent from the maximum. We can fill a building to capacity but cannot keep it filled. We retain about 80 percent of the maximum. After the subtraction, you will find the ASSA (Actual Sunday School Attendance). That is the actual number of people who will attend over a period of time.

Without the information gained from this formula, you will not know how many people you can minister to in your Sunday School building.

You may increase your enrollment, but your Sunday School attendance will remain the same because the space or lack of it places a ceiling on the number of people who can attend. These facts and figures will help utilize the space.

### FIRST BAPTIST CHURCH
*Norfolk, VA*

| ITEM | MAR. '83 | MAR. '90 | INCREASE |
|------|---------|---------|----------|
| Enrollment | 1,085 | 5,616 | 4,531 |
| Prospects | 300 | 1,800 | 1,500 |
| Teaching Units | 33 | 141 | 108 |
| Workers | 112 | 474 | 362 |
| Workers' Mtng. Att. | 0 | 95 | 95 |
| Training Awards | 72 | 90 | 18 |
| Weekly Contacts | NA | 1,904 | 1,904 |
| Outreachers | NA | 70 | 70 |
| SS Attendance | 621 | 2,057 | 1,436 |
| WS Attendance | 752 | 2,849 | 2,097 |
| Weekly Offerings | $7,138 | $47,936 | $40,798 |
| Baptisms | 52 | NA | NA |

# The Church's Ministry Program

*The Value of Contacts*
*The Value of Outreachers*

About the only way a church can do ministry among all of the members and prospects is through the Sunday School. Everyone is assigned to a class or department, and the workers of the teaching units are close enough to the people to discover and minister to their needs.

A contact should be made with every person each week, whether the individual is present or absent. The faithful should be ministered to as well as the unfaithful. Contacts let the people know we care.

Some of the members and prospects do not or cannot attend the church. The best way to minister to these is the personal visit. Both of these methods are essential to minister to the needs of the people. They are done best through the Sunday School.

# 9

# The Value of Contacts

Some people think a Sunday School exists only to teach the Bible. It does, but it does far more. A major part of the Sunday School is meeting the spiritual needs of the members. I know of no other way we can care for these needs unless it is done through the Sunday School. It is organized for this purpose. It has trained personnel to do this.

The Growth Spiral takes this into consideration, as we work toward:

Discovering every prospect.

Enrolling as many as possible.

(When we add these two groups together it gives the total number of people for whom we are responsible at one time.)

Having enough teaching units to care for these.

Having sufficient trained workers to minister to them.

Let us examine contacts. This is the primary method by which the Sunday School does its ministry—contacting, encouraging, praying, evangelizing, and counseling. We have difficulty inducing the Sunday School attendants to report the number of contacts they make each week. Yet, contacts are vitally important to ministry.

Notice on the sample Spiral that sixty contacts are reported each week. Estimate the number of contacts for Sunday School that your people make each week. Insert the number on your Spiral. Be sure to evaluate.

There is a minus in this block on the sample Spiral. With an enrollment of two hundred, sixty contacts each week are not enough. The goal is to have weekly contacts equal to one-half of the Sunday School enrollment. Therefore, the number of contacts should be at least one hundred. Since the enrollment goal is 213 at the end of the first quarter, we need to have at least 106 contacts each week.

As the enrollment increases to 226 at the end of six months, the contacts need to increase to 113. This increases each quarter until there are 252 people enrolled. At that time there needs to be at least 126 contacts every week.

Some think this goal may be too large. But when approximately one-half of the Sunday School enrollment is absent each week, the least we can do is contact those who are absent. This is ministry. People are absent for different reasons. They may be out of town. They may be ill. They may be backslidden. There may be a death or a crisis in the family. Every absence has a reason. Contacts are needed to show them we care. Contacts are primarily for two major reasons.

1. *Ministry.* My wife and I have three children. They are married now and have families of their own. One of our daughters and her husband have four children. When you have that many small ones, there is a strong possibility that each weekend at least one will be sick with a childhood illness.

At the time of this illustration, three of the children were in school. At the beginning of the school year one got the measles and brought the germ home. It seems children don't pass the germ to everyone at the same time. They give it to one child at a time. After the second child goes through the illness, the germ is given to another child and then another, until everyone "enjoys" the agony.

These childhood illnesses, along with several other interruptions, continued for over a two-month period, and they were unable to attend church.

The family was very active, being involved in the music program, Sunday School, missions, and other organizations. It was their custom to be present, and they did so until these illnesses came along.

Not one person from the church contacted them during these weeks! No one visited, telephoned, or wrote a card or letter. Think about this. There were four children in four different classes and a husband and a wife in two other classes. There should have been at least five or six people interested in this family. You guessed correctly—the pastor did not contact them either.

The illnesses came to a close. I asked my daughter and son-in-law what they were going to do. They replied, "We don't know, but we're not going back to that church." Their family is not the kind that thinks the church owes them anything, but our daughter said, "They wouldn't have cared if we had died." It seemed no one cared.

Love, concern, compassion and care must be expressed. One avenue of doing this is through contacts. The contact can be made in several ways: (1) a face-to-face contact; (2) a card or a letter; (3) or a telephone call. *Someone should contact every absentee every week.*

Vary the types of contacts. Sometimes make a phone call. At other times send a card. Sometimes make a pesonal visit, but be sure some kind of contact is made. The more we vary them, the more effective they are.

2. *Increase the attendance.* Here is a formula for increasing the attendance: 1/10/7.

The meaning is simple. There will be an increase in attendance of one when ten contacts are made within seven days of the high attendance day.

If you have one hundred in average attendance now, and you set a high attendance day goal for 125, then you need to make ten personal contacts for each person you want over the average attendance. For a net gain of twenty-five, you need 250 additional contacts within the week. In later chapters, when we study the Sunday School and worship service attendance, we will examine specifics on how to increase these.

*Set Goals for High Attendance*

When we set high-attendance goals, we need to set two goals: a *contact* goal and an *attendance* goal. If we reach the contact goal, the attendance goal is generally met.

An increase in attendance in the Sunday School or worship service is not for the purpose of reaching a goal. That motivation is too low. We increase attendance in order to teach the Bible and minister to more people in the name of the Lord.

Contacts are a vital part of our Bible-teaching ministry. Be sure to complete the Contacts column on your Spiral.

**FIRST SOUTHERN BAPTIST CHURCH**
*Bakersfield, CA*

| ITEM | MAR. '89 | MAR. '90 | INCREASE |
|------|----------|----------|----------|
| Enrollment | 648 | 924 | 276 |
| Prospects | 132 | 294 | 162 |
| Teaching Units | 26 | 51 | 25 |
| Workers | 45 | 135 | 90 |
| Workers' Mtng. Att. | 0 | 75 | 75 |
| Training Awards | 0 | NA | NA |
| Weekly Contacts | 143 | 449 | 306 |
| Outreachers | 0 | 45 | 45 |
| SS Attendance | 290 | 444 | 154 |
| WS Attendance | 320 | 441 | 121 |
| Weekly Offering | $6,467 | $7,328 | $861 |
| Baptisms | 22 | NA | NA |

# 10

# The Value of Outreachers

Look at the Outreachers column on the Spiral. Here is where we place the number of people who participate in the visitation program every week. Write in the average number of participants.

On the sample Spiral there is four, since only four people, on an average, participate in visitation. You will also notice that there is a minus beside this number since there is not enough participation to have a good visitation program. In fact, it is almost a failure.

How can we gain a plus? There should be at least one person visiting weekly from each teaching unit. A teaching unit that does not have someone visiting weekly is failing in its ministry. A plus is received when the number of people in visitation equals the number of teaching units. Those who make telephone calls or write cards and letters are not included as outreachers, only those who place their knuckles on the doors.

There are classes and departments from which no one is visiting. Most of these units are sick because they are not functioning properly.

In order to complete this Outreachers column, I have 11, 12, 13 and 14 because the number of teaching units will be ten during the first quarter, eleven the next, thirteen and then fourteen the last quarter. The Spiral gives us an evaluation method to determine this ministry.

When the Lord led me to minister through the Baptist Sunday School Board more than a decade ago, I began to investigate the visitation programs of our churches. Some have large programs—

hundreds of people visiting every week. I wanted to know how they could have that many people involved in visitation and how they could sustain this program over a period of years.

Here I share the results of these studies.

Two things happen *during* the Sunday School:

1. *Make visitation assignments, during Sunday School, to those who cannot attend the visitation program.* This method is used especially in metropolitan areas. People live so far from their church and work it is impossible for them to come by the church, receive visitation assignments, visit, and return for a report session. So, they receive their assignments during the Sunday School class sessions and make their visits during the week.

Do not make *all* of the assignments during the Sunday School hour. If you do, there will be no stackpole, no day of visitation, and you may lose the entire visitation program. Make only the needed assignments.

2. *Fill out an Outreach Visitation Card during Sunday School.* The Outreach Registration Card can be secured from a local Christian bookstore or by calling 1/800/458-BSSB.

---

**OUTREACH REGISTRATION CARD**

We will represent our class in visitation this week.

1. _____

2. _____

3. _____

4. _____

5. _____

Broadman Supplies 4380-36

---

Attach one of the cards to the class record book which goes into the class. One person in each teaching unit has the responsibility of securing people to commit themselves for the visitation program.

Almost without exception someone in the class will say, "I'll visit if someone will go with me." Ordinarily, at least two people sign up.

For instance, if there are eight teaching units in the Sunday School and you use this card, there is an excellent possibility that sixteen people will visit this week. Sixteen people visiting is much better than the four we have on the sample Spiral. Instead of having a minus, we have a plus, but more important is the personal, spiritual ministry to the people.

In the churches where this card is effectively used, the visitation attendance increases significantly. When people commit themselves to do something, most of the time they will follow through.

If possible, in the worship service, the pastor should make the announcement about visitation. He needs to lead the visitation program. There are precious few successful visitation programs that are not led by the pastor. This should be one of his priorities. He does not have to do all of the work in planning for this program, only lead it. Once he makes this commitment, he places himself in the position of leadership. Other people should be assigned to set it up.

*Properly Set Up for Visitation*

Use the *Reach Out Outreach Pocket and Card* in your visitation program. This card, developed many years ago, is one of the best visitation programs in existence today. Three books (packets) of these cards should be prepared for *each* class and department.

On the visitation day, have a table for each teaching unit. If you do not have that many tables, perhaps you can use a table for two or more teaching units.

*Visitation Book 1*

Complete a *Reach Out Pocket and Card* for every person enrolled in each teaching unit. Let us assume that one table is set up for a class of adult men which has twenty pupils enrolled. Therefore, in book #1 we have twenty *Reach Out Pocket and Cards*.

Remove the cards from all of the envelopes and place them on one end of the table. The reason we place *all* of the cards on the table, and not just those who were absent last Sunday, is fundamental. *We do not believe in absentee visitation. We believe in ministry visitation.*

Absentee visitation will kill the visitation program because the same people seem to be absent each week. As a result, we ask our people to visit the same people every week. When these absentees find out the night we visit, they close the drapes, turn off the television, and wait for us to come and go. We drive them away.

Also, our people stop visiting if the only people they have to visit are the absentees. This does not mean that absentees should not be visited. They should, but they should not consume all of the visitation.

The twenty men who are enrolled in this adult men's class need to be contacted. Someone needs to visit those who are present every week and say, "We thank the Lord for you and your faithfulness." This is *ministry* visitation.

### Visitation Book 2

Book #2 is composed of the enrollment prospects. We need as many prospects for enrollment as we have people who are enrolled. With twenty men enrolled in the sample class, we need at least twenty enrollment prospects. Remove these cards and place them on the table. During the visitation program, these enrollment prospects should be contacted and invited to enroll. This places a major emphasis on *enrollment.*

### Visitation Book 3

Book #3 is made up of *evangelistic* prospects for this class. The preschool and younger children's departments do not have book #3 because the children have not reached the age of accountability and are not evangelistic prospects.

Remove the cards from the envelopes and place them on the table. There may be some duplications in this book (packet). Some class members or prospects may also be unsaved, and are also listed in this book. This places a special emphasis on them—they need to be enrolled in Bible study *and* evangelized.

### A Visitation Meal

More than one-half of the ladies in the churches work outside of their homes. After they work eight hours, pick up the children from day care, prepare the evening meal, clean up following the meal, bathe and dress the children, and drive to the church for visitation, they are too exhausted to participate. If they do not attend, their husbands are often absent also. In pilot churches, where a meal has been provided, attendance has increased considerably. This meal should *not* be a banquet, more like soup and salad or cold cuts.

Before the people have completed the meal, the pastor should spend a few minutes motivating the attenders. He could say something like, "We don't visit because our denominational leaders say we ought to visit. We visit because 'thus saith the Lord.'"

At this point he could read one of the many verses which challenge the people and conclude with, "I am going out of that door to visit, and I want you to go with me." The people will follow their leader.

Once they have been challenged, the people go to their table and make their visitation selections. They are not locked into one type of visitation.

(1) They may visit an absentee or another member of the class.

(2) They may visit for the purpose of enrolling someone in Sunday School.

(3) If they are evangelistically trained, they may choose to share a soul-winning witness.

Once they accept their assignment, they make their visit and return for a report session.

One of the most important parts of the visitation program is to have the evangelism visitation simultaneously with the rest of the visitation. People who concentrate on ministry or absentee visitation usually do not return motivated. Those who visit to enroll people in Sunday School may not come back motivated. They may return demotivated. But the evangelists are *always* highly motivated. They are the *generators* who put enthusiasm into all of the visitors. Following the report session, everyone is excited and can hardly wait until the next visitation session.

Visitation is primary. Visitation is ministry. Visitation is enrolling. Visitation is evangelism. Establish a good visitation program. Place the statistics on your Spiral.

**FIRST BAPTIST CHURCH**
*New Baden, IL*

| ITEM | OCT. '83 | OCT. '90 | INCREASE |
|---|---|---|---|
| Enrollment | 15 | 415 | 400 |
| Prospects | 0 | 212 | 212 |
| Teaching Units | 2 | 21 | 19 |
| Workers | 2 | 44 | 42 |
| Workers' Mtng. Att. | 0 | 35 | 35 |
| Training Awards | 0 | 60 | 60 |
| Weekly Contacts | 10 | 260 | 250 |
| Outreachers | 1 | 21 | 20 |
| SS Attendance | 8 | 180 | 172 |
| WS Attendance | 12 | 210 | 198 |
| Weekly Offering | $95 | $2,380 | $2,275 |
| Baptisms | 0 | 22 | 22 |

# The Church's Bible Teaching Program

## Enlarged Bible Teaching Attendance

The Sunday School is designed for quality Bible teaching. It is the only organization designed to teach the Bible to each age group each week.

The projection of future attendance enables the leadership to plan for expansion. The use of the law of cause and effect is the basis on which these figures rest.

# 11

# Enlarged Bible Teaching Attendance

There are four projections on the Spiral. One deals with Sunday School attendance, one with worship attendance, one with offerings, and one with baptisms.

The column labeled Sunday School Attendance on the sample Spiral reveals how we use the "law of cause and effect" to project attendance.

With an enrollment of two hundred, there is an average attendance of seventy-five. This indicates that only 38 percent of the enrollment is average in attendance. This evaluation results in a minus, since less than 40 percent of the enrollment is average in attendance.

*The evaluation on the sample Spiral reveals the reason why the attendance is so low. Every minus is a weakness.* Though we may know of these weaknesses, the Spiral points a finger at each. We also know how severe the weakness is.

The Spiral is designed to change the minuses into pluses. It is imperative that we increase the quality of Bible teaching as we reach additional people. At the end of the year, if all of the minuses are changed to pluses, the Christian education program will be much stronger than it is now. If this happens the Sunday School attendance will increase to at least 45 percent of the projected enrollment. With 250 people enrolled at the end of the year the projection is that at least 113 people will be in attendance.

Do not be discouraged if you do not meet your goals each

quarter. In most churches, there are two growth quarters and two non-growth quarters.

For instance, in South Florida where I pastored, our growth quarters were in the fall and winter when people came to visit with us. Growth quarters are not the same throughout the United States. Church leaders know which of the quarters are growth and non-growth. In this book we will use a straight line increase, considering each quarter equally. On the sample Spiral the attendance has increased during the year from seventy-five, which is 38 percent of the enrollment, to 113, 45 percent of the enrollment. This is a result of the law of cause and effect.

This law is used to make these four projections. This is God's law. We use it every minute of every day. When I prepare to drive my car, I place the key in the ignition, turn it on, and the engine starts—cause and effect.

At mealtime I lift the fork, on which I have placed the food, to my mouth. That is the cause. Ummm, good taste is the effect. We live by this law all of the time.

Since the law belongs to the Lord and the church belongs to Him, its accuracy within the church can be depended upon. As we equally increase the quantity, the quality and the ministry, we can project the attendance in our Sunday School.

Refer to the chapter on workers to see how the ratio of workers to enrollment affects the attendance. Also, a lack of space is like a vise. It will hold you in its grip and choke the very life out of the church growth. It deals with the formula I gave you in the chapter on space. That formula is:

TOTAL SQUARE FEET divided by 40 = MSSA _____
(Maximum Sunday School Attendance)

Subtract 20% = ASSA _____
(Actual Sunday School Attendance)

Discover your total square feet of educational space. Measure the outside of your educational space. Divide the total amount of square feet by 40 square feet, because experience has shown us that this is the amount needed for each person in attendance.

That sounds like a lot. I am six feet tall. From the fingertips on one hand to the fingertips of the other is approximately six feet. I can stand in one place, rotate my body, and cover approximately 36 square feet. Therefore, 40 square feet isn't much to allow for each person.

You may comment, "A person can sit in a lot less space than that." Right. But the 40 square feet includes all of the support areas: the hallways, the stairs, the rest rooms, assembly rooms, and maintenance rooms, etc.

Once you have decided the square feet in the educational area and have divided it by 40 square feet, you have discovered the maximum Sunday School attendance. It is impossible to keep a maximum attendance. People will not sit shoulder to shoulder for an indefinite period of time. They need some slouching room. Again, experience has shown us that we must subtract 20 percent from the maximum Sunday School attendance. This shows what your average or actual attendance will be.

Once you find your (ASSA), Actual Sunday School Attendance, compare it with your present Sunday School attendance, and you will probably discover that you have already reached your saturation attendance. This reveals when you need to expand to a second or third Sunday School or find space outside of your building. This is a valuable column in long-range planning.

When you set attendance goals, keep in mind the amount of space available for attendance. Be sure that you have quality Bible study for the people when they attend Sunday School.

A friend of mine tells a story of how his father raised pigs. He poured the swill into a hollowed-out tree that formed the trough for the hog food. Then he beat on the side of the hollow log with a stick. The hogs responded to the sound. That was their dinner bell. This worked well until some woodpeckers came through, sat on the hollow log, and b-r-r-t, b-r-r-r-t. The hogs came, but there was no food. Even after his dad killed the woodpeckers, the hogs would not return because they had been fooled too many times.

I am not drawing the conclusion that people who come to Sunday School are hogs, but I hope that illustration reminds us to feed the people when they attend. There must be spiritual nourishment for them.

Be sure to place your average Sunday School attendance on your Spiral and discover your percentage. If you discovered that your average attendance is more than 60 percent of your enrollment, you may be in serious trouble. There are some exceptions, but most churches will average between 40 percent and 60 percent in attendance. If your church is relatively new, small, or if it is located in a rural setting, the attendance may be 60 percent or higher.

Surveys show us it is almost impossible to sustain a percentage of 60 percent or higher. Usually, it is because someone is cleaning the Sunday School roll in order to keep a high attendance.

The average attendance in the Southern Baptist Convention (the largest Sunday School enrollment in the world) runs about 48 percent to 49 percent of the enrollment. Again, keep in mind that the logistics of the society in which we live keep about one-half of the enrollees absent each week. About the only way I know to keep a high percentage of the enrollment in attendance is to erase the names of people who are irregular. But that is most detrimental.

Here is a law we can depend on if good Sunday School principles are practiced:

- When the enrollment increases the attendance increases.
- When the enrollment decreases the attendance deceases.

**ALPHA BAPTIST CHURCH**
*Aurora, CO*

| ITEM | OCT. '88 | MAR. '90 | INCREASE |
|---|---|---|---|
| Enrollment | 40 | 240 | 200 |
| Prospects | 20 | 75 | 55 |
| Teaching Units | 6 | 14 | 8 |
| Workers | 8 | 20 | 12 |
| Workers' Mtng. Att. | 4 | 14 | 10 |
| Training Awards | 0 | 6 | 6 |
| Weekly Contacts | 25 | 80 | 55 |
| Outreachers | 2 | 9 | 7 |
| SS Attendance | 40 | 110 | 70 |
| WS Attendance | 55 | 115 | 60 |
| Weekly Offering | $250 | $4,001 | $3,751 |
| Baptisms | 9 | 27 | 18 |

# The Church's Worship Ministry

## *Increased Worship Service Attendance*

The Spiral is designed to assist the leadership in planning for increased worship attendance. By knowing the seating capacity of the worship center, it is possible to discern in advance when there is a need for multiple worship services. The Spiral becomes a planning tool.

# 12

# Increased Worship Service Attendance

The worship service attendance can also be projected. In the sample Spiral there is an average of eighty-five people in the morning worship service. We have found the most accurate projection is: the numerical difference between the Sunday School and worship attendance will remain about the same.

For instance, I have ten more people in worship than in Sunday School. At the end of the first quarter, there will probably be about ten more people in worship than in Sunday School. That will likely continue throughout the year.

In the sample Spiral, the pastor who is preaching to eighty-five people will be preaching to 123 people one year from now, provided he becomes involved with his Sunday School and works his ministry through it.

As the Sunday School attendance increases, the worship service will also. Look at it from the other side. If the Sunday School attendance decreases, the worship service usually will decrease.

The best way to have a larger attendance in the worship service is to do it through the Sunday School. If the worship service attendance is developed through the ministry of the Sunday School, the attendance will not be greatly affected when the pastor moves to another church. Then the attendance is built around the total ministry of the church. Some pastors, of course, are gifted and dynamic. Great numbers attend their worship services, even if there is not a great Sunday School, but another fact is to be considered. There is a difference between a morning worship service and a New Testament church. A pastor is called to develop a New Testament church, which is reaching, evangelizing, and discipling (Matt. 28:19-20). The people who attend a worship service *only* do not ordinarily become involved in outreach visitation, personal soul-winning, and discipleship.

In Psalm 29:2 the Bible reminds us that we should "Worship the Lord in the beauty of holiness" (worship service), but it also says in 2 Timothy 2:15 that we should "Study to show thyself approved unto God" (Sunday School). A Christian needs both of these experiences to grow into being a complete follower of Christ.

When the pastor can reach people through his ability to preach God's Word, it is his responsibility to lead them into the systemized Bible study program. They are benefited by the small teaching unit for fellowship, study, involvement, discipleship, and ministry. Also, when the Sunday School functions properly, it should support the worship service.

Some churches should restudy their worship services. In some cases the order of service should be altered. Instead of beginning every service with a call to worship, an invocation followed by two songs and a prayer, two more songs, and the announcements, the leaders should give spiritual thought and prayer to making the worship experience more meaningful. Do not change the order of service simply for the sake of change, but it is helpful to adjust the elements so the service will be more uplifting to the worshipers.

I was in a service not long ago that illustrates this point. Following the call to worship and the invocation, the choir sang. It was as if heaven came down! It was one of those times when the Holy Spirit made a special visit. The pastor could have given an invitation at that moment, but didn't. Instead he stepped to the pulpit and began the sermon. We had not been in the service more than four or five minutes, and he was already preaching. You should have seen the reaction from the worshipers. I could hear people whispering to one another, "He has never done this before," and, "We haven't received the offering yet."

The pastor changed the order of the service because he felt the leading of the Spirit. Why not? After the sermon and the invitation, the announcements were made, the offering received, and the service concluded. I have been in many worship services which I have forgotten, but I will never forget that one.

I was in another unforgettable service. The pastor preached on the "prodigal sons." After he had preached for ten minutes on the subject of the first son, he gave an invitation. Do you know what I thought? *Wow, we had a short sermon!* But I was mistaken. After the invitation hymn was completed, we sat down, and the pastor completed his sermon by preaching on the second son for an additional ten minutes. This was followed by a second invitation. Change can be helpful.

The order of service should be designed to make the worship service a time when the people deeply sense the presence of God. The music in the worship service should be as well planned as the sermon.

The service should be a celebration. Why? Because Sunday is the day we celebrate the resurrection of our Lord. When we assemble on Sunday it is because the Lord rose from the dead on the first day of the week. Yet, there are churches where the music sounds like a funeral dirge. Since about one-half of the worship service is given to music, it should be played and sung in celebration. I am not talking about new music or rhythm or hand-clapping.

The grand hymns of the church, such as "Holy, Holy, Holy," "How Firm a Foundation" and others, are among the greatest songs ever written, and they are usable today in our services. They are as uplifting and celebrative as "contemporary" Christian music. It is not merely the songs that lift, but it is how we sing and play the songs.

What about the announcements? It is a puzzle why we spend so much time and effort to have a meaningful worship experience only to shut down for five to ten minutes for announcements. I do not know what to do with them, but we should keep them out of the middle of the service. One thing which helped in my last pastorate was when we decided that no announcement would be made publicly that did not relate to the whole church. If the information was printed in the bulletin, it was not necessary to repeat it from the pulpit. We also moved the announcements to the beginning of the hour, before the call to worship.

More expository preaching is called for. The Bible instructs us to "preach the word." When I first became a pastor, most of my sermons were topical. I would select a topic, develop an outline, find a few interesting illustrations, do some research, and then pray over it.

What I discovered was frightening. I could prepare a topical sermon without ever opening my Bible. People are not often saved through topical sermons. The Bible reminds us "Being born again, . . . by the word of God" (1 Pet. 1:23). The Word of God must be preached and not simply the ideas of the preacher.

During my twenty-year pastorate at Riverside Baptist Church, Fort Myers, Florida, I had the privilege to preach through the entire Bible and almost halfway through it a second time. I did not start with Genesis and go straight through to The Revelation because perhaps some of my people would have died before I reached the New Testament. I alternated between the Old and New Testament. One of my pastor friends reported that he preached through the Bible like that, and after a while his people, in talking with one another, remarked, "I joined during 2 Corinthians. When did you join?" "Oh, I joined during Psalms," etc. What an exciting testimony!

More and more pastors ought to preach the Bible chapter by chapter, verse by verse, and, if possible, word by word. When it is preached expositorily and exegetically, the man of God is forced to spend more time studying and meditating.

When I first started preaching, I spent considerable time trying to find subjects to preach. But once the decision was made to preach through the books of the Bible I never had to hunt for material to preach. It is imperative to have a Bible-teaching program and a worship experience that touch God and man. The invitation at the conclusion of the service should be Spirit-led, simple, and practical. Some in attendance may need to accept Jesus as Savior, others need to unite with the membership of the church, and some may need to rededicate their lives to Christ. Give them an opportunity to do all these.

Each person involved in the visitation program of our church carried *Applications for Church Membership* cards. When a person is led to Christ, we encouraged him or her to fill out the card in their home. They brought the completed card when they attended the next worship service. This made it easier for them to make a public decision. Filling out the card did not make them a member of the church but made it easier for them to follow through with their decision.

This column on the Spiral is one of the most important projections. Grow the Sunday School attendance, and it will help grow the worship service attendance. Grow the worship service attendance, and it will help grow the Sunday School attendance.

## PERIMETER ROAD BAPTIST CHURCH
*Valdosta, GA*

| ITEM | MAR. '87 | MAR. '90 | INCREASE |
|------|----------|----------|----------|
| Enrollment | 0 | 550 | 550 |
| Prospects | 0 | 331 | 331 |
| Teaching Units | 0 | 22 | 22 |
| Workers | 0 | 59 | 59 |
| Workers' Mtng. Att. | 0 | 17 | 17 |
| Training Awards | 0 | 50 | 50 |
| Weekly Contacts | 0 | 108 | 108 |
| Outreachers | 0 | 26 | 26 |
| SS Attendance | 0 | 261 | 261 |
| WS Attendance | 0 | 304 | 304 |
| Weekly Offerings | 0 | $4,016 | $4,016 |
| Baptisms | 0 | 43 | 43 |

# The Church's Stewardship Ministry

## *Increased Offerings*

We reach people like us. As we grow, we reach people who have the same basic income. By discovering the per capita income of the church, as explained in this chapter, it is possible to project the future income. The per capita remains about the same.

Of course, the biblical teachings concerning God's plan of church finance must be taught to the new members.

# 13

# Increased Offerings

Let us examine how this column helps us to make projections concerning the finances of the church. In the column labeled *offerings*, $750 has been recorded as the total weekly, undesignated receipts. Some of these tithes and offerings came through the Sunday School, some through the worship services, some on Wednesday evening, and others may have been mailed in—but the average per week was $750.

On the sample Spiral, I have placed $10 pcg. This is the per capita giving. We arrived at this figure by dividing the average Sunday School attendance into the offering. When 75 is divided into the $750, the total weekly, undesignated offering, the result is $10 per person attending. This includes every bed baby, child, youth and adult.

There are other ways to figure the per capita giving. We could divide the worship service attendance into the offering. However, we have discovered in our surveys that, on an average, persons who attend the worship service *only*, place about 50 cents a week in the offering plate. It is very difficult to make a projection on 50 cents a week. We could divide the Sunday School enrollment into the offerings, and that would give us another per capita giving figure. The major problem with this is that about one-half of the Sunday School enrollment is absent. How can we adequately project a per capita giving by working with absentees?

We found that the most accurate, projectable figure comes by dividing the Sunday School attendance into the offering. This becomes a most important statistic in budget planning. On an average, $10 will be brought by each person in attendance at Sunday School.

As we grow, we reach people who are like us. If you have a per capita giving of $10 now, the new people you enroll will probably give the same per capita. If your people are giving $8 or $7 per capita now, the new people will probably give the same. If your people are giving $20 per capita now, the new people will probably give $20 per capita. The point is, as we grow, we reach people who respond like us.

As the projection for Sunday School attendance continues to increase from seventy-five the first quarter to eighty-five the second quarter, the offering will be eighty-five times $10 per capita, or $850 per week.

By the end of six months, with ninety-four people in attendance in Sunday School, the offering will be ninety-four times $10 per capita or $940 per week. It will continue so that by the end of the year, with 113 in attendance, the offering will be $1,130 every week. That's quite a jump from $750.

I know that certain people will think that's silly, that it won't work. Yet, we are finding in our conferences that the per capita giving does not decrease as we grow but increases. We are excited about what the Lord is doing with the income. This is how it should be. God is under no obligation to underwrite a Christian club. He is only under obligation to underwrite a New Testament church.

A Christian club is a church which does not carry out the Great Commission, going, evangelizing and discipling—and does not grow. When a church is in a nongrowth posture, how does it garner additional income? The money, God's tithes and offerings, comes from people in attendance. If the attendance does not increase, the offerings do not. The cost of living continues to rise, but the offerings do not rise as fast. As a result, over a period of time, the church will be in financial trouble.

One of the first things I see taking place in this situation is that we cut back on the literature order. We argue that we cannot provide quarterlies to all of the members. However, Philippians 4:19 says that "God shall supply all your need."

We should not blame people for not giving. They are probably giving as much as they have always given. The problem is that the cost of living is rising, but the income is not rising. Thus, we have a financial shortage and cut back on mission giving. Instead of the 12 percent we've always given, we reduce it to 11 percent, and then we cut back to 10 percent. We must see that this deficiency is a caution flag waving over the church, screaming, "Something is wrong."

God's Word tells us that if we will carry out the Great Commission, He will supply our every need. What is the Great Commission? We are to go into all the world and teach the Bible evangelistically, baptizing those who are won to Christ, and then discipling them. There are three major actions in this commission: outreach, evangelism and discipleship. If we reach the people, evangelize and disciple them, through them God provides all of the money we need.

If we don't have all the money we need, it is evident that we are not carrying out the Great Commission as we should. As we reach more people, God will supply additional money through them. If we do not reach additional people, we will not have additional money.

It doesn't matter what words are on the church marquee, the bulletin board, or what we place on our stationery. We can call ourselves a church until we are blue in the face, but unless we are carrying out the Great Commission—reaching, evangelizing and discipling—we are not a church but a Christian club.

Approximately six thousand churches in the United States close their doors every year and go out of business. I made that statement in a classroom where a man challenged me with, "The Bible says the gates of hell cannot prevail against the church. How is it that six thousand die each year?" The reason is that they are not fulfilling the Great Commission. They are not New Testament-type churches. The Lord has no obligation to keep their doors open. Let me show you a diagram which will explain how to have all of the money you need in your church.

$$\frac{95}{\smash{\big)}\,\$950.00}\;\$10.00$$

First, make a division box. Inside write your *weekly financial needs*. How much does your church need every week to do all it needs to do? That's probably a larger figure than you have ever thought about, but think it through. Make a guess. How much does your church need every week to do *everything* you need to do? Write that figure inside of the division box where I have placed $950. Now, divide the per capita giving figure you discovered earlier in this chapter into the weekly financial needs. In my illustration I divide $10 into the weekly financial needs. The result is the number of people needed in attendance in Sunday School each week.

When you have that many people attending Sunday School, they will bring the per capita amount, and you will have all of the money you need to do everything you need to do. God will provide the financial needs.

If you do not have enough money to meet the needs of the church, this is not the time to preach on stewardship. Preach on it later. If you do not have enough to meet your budget, the interpretation of your sermon by the pew is "Give, because we need money to pay the bills." The Bible says nothing about people tithing in order to pay the church debt. We tithe to grow spiritually and to be obedient to God. If there is not enough income, enroll some people in Sunday School. It sounds foolish, but it works.

Look again at the sample Spiral. About one-half of the Sunday School enrollment is average in attendance. So if your per capita giving is $10, as mine is, and you need $10 more per week, enroll two people in Sunday School and care for their needs. One of them will attend and give $10.

If you are $100 short per week, enroll twenty people and meet their needs. Ten of them will attend, each one will bring $10, and you will have $100 additional money. The point is that the Great Commission is God's plan to keep us busy doing what we are supposed to do. The Lord has said for us to carry out His Commission, and He will give us all we need. But, if we don't carry out the Great Commission, He may let us die.

God is not short of money. All we have to do is show Him we are interested in reaching, evangelizing, discipling and teaching people.

### COUNTRY AND TOWN BAPTIST CHURCH
*Mechanicsburg, PA*

| ITEM | MAR. '85 | MAR. '90 | INCREASE |
|---|---|---|---|
| Enrollment | 316 | 695 | 379 |
| Prospects | NA | 450 | 450 |
| Teaching Units | 18 | 35 | 17 |
| Workers | 45 | 85 | 40 |
| Workers' Mtng. Att. | 0 | 40 | 40 |
| Training Awards | 0 | 66 | 66 |
| Weekly Contacts | 25 | 400 | 375 |
| Outreachers | 6 | 10 | 4 |
| SS Attendance | 145 | 294 | 149 |
| WS Attendance | 210 | 450 | 240 |
| Weekly Offering | $2,650 | $8,000 | $5,350 |
| Baptisms | 22 | 43 | 19 |

# The Church's Evangelism Ministry

## Increased Evangelism

There is no definite projection of the increase in baptisms, however, most of the churches using the Spiral will double the evangelism results during the first year.

The Spiral reflects the effectiveness of this primary work.

# 14

# Increased Evangelism

Churches using the Growth Spiral, on an average, double their baptisms during the first year.

On the sample Spiral notice I have placed 3 in the Baptisms block. We have been averaging three baptisms a year. Under normal circumstances, if we properly use the Spiral, we will increase baptisms. Winning people to Jesus Christ is still the most important mission of the church.

We are discovering that when we use open enrollment, about one-half of the people we enroll are unsaved. But we are not surprised—far more than one-half of the world is unsaved. Of course, we cannot enroll all of them, but experience indicates we can enroll many if we honestly try.

If we increase the enrollment by fifty-two during the year, as the sample Spiral indicates, there is an excellent possibility that twenty-six of the new people will be unsaved.

About one-half of our enrollment attends regularly; so with twenty-six *unsaved* people enrolled during the year, it is probable that thirteen of these *unsaved* people will be in attendance each week.

The Bible is taught in the classes where the love of God is presented. They attend the worship service where there is an invitation to accept Jesus as Savior. Surveys show thirteen will be saved and baptized within the year. That does not mean the thirteen unsaved people we enrolled will be saved, but an equal number will come to know the Lord as Savior.

We believe in quality Bible teaching, quality ministry and quality discipleship. However, the priority of the Sunday School is evangelism. It is urgent that the unsaved be enrolled in Bible study. Evangelism is best done through the Sunday School.

Here are our findings:

1. The best methods for discovering evangelistic prospects are through the Sunday School.
2. One-half of the people we enroll in Sunday School are unsaved.
3. One out of two unsaved people *whom we enroll* in Sunday School will be saved and baptized in a year.
4. One out of about four hundred unsaved people *whom we do not enroll* in Sunday School will be saved and baptized in twelve months.
5. After a person has been enrolled in Sunday School and then led to Christ, assimilation into the church membership is almost 100 percent.
6. Discipleship is much more successful when the new convert is involved in a small Bible class.
   —Through the Sunday School classes we found the prospects.
   —Through the Sunday School classes we won and evangelized the prospects.
   —Through the Sunday School classes we discipled the prospects.

Enroll the lost, and get them in Sunday School. Train every teacher to be a soul winner, and evangelism is the result. Churches with growing Sunday Schools are baptizing about ten times more people than average churches.

May this be the greatest year you've ever had for the Lord Jesus Christ.

**COOK BAPTIST CHURCH**
*Ruston, LA*

| ITEM | MAR. '86 | MAR. '90 | INCREASE |
|---|---|---|---|
| Enrollment | 634 | 1,364 | 730 |
| Prospects | 200 | 1,175 | 975 |
| Teaching Units | 25 | 71 | 46 |
| Workers | 48 | 141 | 93 |

| ITEM | MAR. '86 | MAR. '90 | INCREASE |
|---|---|---|---|
| Workers' Mtng. Att. | 12 | 85 | 73 |
| Training Awards | 0 | 40 | 40 |
| Weekly Contacts | NA | 500 | 500 |
| Outreachers | NA | 80 | 80 |
| SS Attendance | 303 | 558 | 255 |
| WS Attendance | 400 | 530 | 130 |
| Weekly Offering | $6,116 | $8,000 | $1,884 |
| Baptisms | 0 | 111 | 111 |

# The Church's Age-Group Development

*The Adult Spiral*
*The Youth Spiral*
*The Children's Spiral*
*The Preschool Spiral*

The educational program of a church is organized into four age groups: Adult, Youth, Children and Preschool.

The next four chapters are designed to assist the age-group leaders to design Growth Spirals for their classes and departments.

Quantity, quality and ministry must be administered through every teaching unit.

# 15

# The Adult Spiral

## Interpretation

In the back of the book you will find a completed Adult Sunday School Growth Spiral. Look at it now, and follow it during the reading of this chapter.

## Quantity

Begin the Adult Spiral with the date of the quarter (10/1, 1/1, 4/1, or 7/1) that is closest. The sample Spiral has been started with 10/1.

*Enrollment*

The present enrollment of the adult class (unit) is placed in the first block. On the sample Spiral you will notice that the present enrollment in this unit is twenty-five. I have placed a plus ( + ) under this column because the recommended maximum enrollment for an adult class is twenty-five. The best size for a growing adult unit is less than twenty-five, however.

Now, a yearly enrollment goal will need to be set for the adult unit. A yearly goal of eight has been set for the sample Spiral. Since a quarterly goal (three months) is more easily reached, that goal has been divided by four. A goal of two adults enrolled every three months has been set, and the additional blocks on the sample Spiral have been filled out under the enrollment column.

On 1/1 there will be 27 adults enrolled. On 4/1, 29. By 7/1, 31, and by 10/1 of the following year, 33.

Note: When you actually reach the maximum recommended enrollment goal for an adult unit (25) you would start a new unit. Then, you would make out new Spirals for the two classes. Since this is a teaching Spiral, not an actual adult class, I will complete the year on one Spiral as an example.

*Prospects*

Place the number of valid adult prospects in the first block on the Adult Spiral. A valid prospect is an adult for whom you have a name, address, phone number and age. On the sample Spiral there are twenty-five adult prospects for this class. I have placed a minus (-) under the prospect column because the number of prospects needs to equal the number of adults enrolled in order for this class to grow.

One of the primary reasons for nongrowth is the lack of valid prospects.

## Quality

*Teaching Units*

When you fill out a Spiral for your own adult class (unit) you will place a 1 in this column as I have on the sample Spiral, because this Spiral is for one class or unit.

Notice that as I move up the Spiral the enrollment is divided by 25 (maximum recommended enrollment). By 1/1, two units are needed. After those two units have been started no new units need be started for the rest of the year unless the enrollment in either class exceeds twenty-five again.

A plus has been placed under the Units column because on 10/1 the maximum enrollment for one unit did not exceed twenty-five.

*Workers*

Each new class needs one worker for every five adults enrolled. On the sample Spiral there are five workers for this class, thus, a plus (5 workers + 20 adults = 25 enrolled). The workers are: one teacher, one outreach leader, and three group (care) leaders.

Remember, when you move up the Spiral and the enrollment increases, the number of workers needed increases.

*Workers' Meeting*

Adult workers reach people for Bible study, teach the Bible, witness to persons about Christ, lead persons into church membership, minister to people in need, encourage people to worship and support the ministry of the church. Because of these important tasks, adult workers need a time to come together to plan for these ministries.

Three-fourths of the adult workers in each class need to be in attendance in a workers' meeting on a regular basis. Since there are five workers on 10/1 on the sample Spiral, at least four of these workers need to be in attendance to obtain a plus under this column. Four workers do attend on a regular basis, thus, a plus under this column.

*Training Awards*

Because the tasks of the adult workers are so important they also must be trained to be the best possible adult workers. Training awards should equal at least one-half the number of workers in an adult class each quarter.

On the sample Spiral the adult class received two training awards in the last three months; therefore a minus has been placed under the Training Awards column. One-half of five workers means that class needed three training awards in the past three months.

## Outreach/Ministry

*Space*

Count the number of possible spaces available for adult classes to meet. Hopefully there will be enough spaces for each adult class and some extra for anticipated growth. Place that number in the first block under Units.

*Contacts*

Contacts are cards, letters, visits or phone calls. These contacts need to be made on a weekly basis. This and the outreachers column are the only columns on the Spiral that are weekly goals. Contacts cannot wait three months (a quarter); they must be made on a weekly basis.

A plus here requires contacts each week equaling at least half the number enrolled in a class. "That many?" you may ask. Yes. A class of twenty-five adults may have only ten or twelve who attend regularly. Those who do not attend need to be contacted. By the way, those adults who do attend need to be contacted also—thus, the need for contacts to equal at least one-half the number of adults enrolled. Remember, as the enrollment increases as you move up the Spiral, the number of weekly contacts needs to increase. Five contacts were made last week—on the sample Spiral, a minus.

*Outreachers*

Outreachers are adult workers who are reaching out to others in visitation. The goal is to have at least one from each adult class visiting each week. A plus has been placed on the sample Spiral under this column because one worker from this class visited last week.

## Projections

*Sunday School Attendance*

The present average Sunday School attendance goes in the first block under the Sunday School Attendance column. Twelve (12) has been placed here on the sample Spiral. A minus has also been placed here because at least one-half of the Sunday School enrollment needs to be present on a regular basis for a plus. One-half of 25 is 13, thus a minus.

*Worship Service Attendance*

At least one-half of the Sunday School enrollment also needs to be in attendance for the worship service to merit a plus. On the sample Spiral this class has a plus because fifteen of the twenty-five enrolled are in attendance in the worship service.

*Offerings*

Place the quarterly offerings received from the adults in your class in the first block. You can project future offerings by dividing the offerings by the number of adults attending to get the per capita giving.

*Baptisms*

The number of baptisms from your adult class last quarter go in this block. Goals can be set for baptisms each quarter. Adult workers: use the Adult Sunday School Growth Spiral to reach, teach, minister and witness to adults more effectively.

## Implementation

### Your Adult Classes' Outreach Ministry

*Finding and Enrolling Adult Prospects*

Finding and enrolling adults does not just happen. Adult workers need to plan and organize to reach and enroll adults.

—One of the best ways to begin is to update or start a prospect file. You might want to begin with 3 x 5 cards distributed to all workers and adult members. Ask these adults to place the name, address, phone number, and age of any prospects they know on these cards.

—Look over the present prospect information you have. Is it up to date? Write letters or cards to these prospects at least once a month. Call them. Visit them.

—Obtain a list of all unenrolled church members. Prepare prospect cards on all of them. Try to enroll them in Sunday School, weekday Bible study, or other Bible study programs your church may have. You may want to transfer them to the Sunday School class where they would belong if they were members, so someone will be responsible to minister to them.

—Make a list of all the unenrolled parents of children, preschoolers or youth that are enrolled.

—Get a list of all guests (visitors) in the worship service. Call them that afternoon. Send a letter to them on Monday. Try to visit them within three days of their visit.

—Get the names of new people who have moved to your community through the utility companies, Welcome Wagon, etc.

—Assign adults to watch the block where they live for any newcomers. Visit new families when they move into homes on the block. Take food baskets from the church or the adult Sunday School

classes. Leave something that must be returned to the church with directions to the church. When that person returns the item, give them a tour and information about the church and the adult Sunday School.
—Visit house to house. Use open enrollment. Enroll adults anytime, anyplace, as long as they agree.
—Use a people search, an inside-the-church survey, enroll church members, use I Know a Prospect cards, real estate sales, Family Life Center (if your church has one), and people you know.

Adult prospects are all around you. Seek them out, enroll them, minister to them and witness to them.

## Your Adult Classes' Organizational Program

*Finding Additional Adult Space*

All growing churches find it difficult to locate additional spaces for adults to meet. This should not deter adults from finding and enrolling prospects. Adults need to develop creative ways to find additional space.

Adults are more flexible than some of the other age groups and can meet in places where others cannot.

—Try meeting in portable buildings, the choir loft, balcony or worship center.
—What about RV's, vans or buses?
—Think about adjacent businesses, stores, homes, schools or malls.
—Think about the adult men's class that meets in the funeral home and calls itself the Lazarus Class. Creative? Yes. You can be too.
—Use round tables in the fellowship hall. Each table becomes a "class."
—Use movable partitions in large rooms and portable chalkboards. Use stackable chairs.
—Try the church foyer, the prayer room, bride's room, church offices, library or media center.
—Encourage your church to have multiple Sunday Schools.
—Plan Bible study on days or nights other than Sunday morning.
—Begin classes for single adults, unmarried college students, deaf

or hearing-impaired adults, visually impaired, physically handicapped, non-English speaking adults, mentally retarded adults,
homebound or nursing home adults, adults away or those from
other cultures.

Adult classes should always be growing. Keep classes small to
effectively reach, teach, witness, minister, and win all the adults
possible.

## Your Adult Classes' Discipleship Ministry

*Finding Adult Workers*

Adult workers are special people. An adult worker can be any
member of the church who is willing to be involved, have acceptable standards, and to use the special gifts and talents God has
given him or her.

Pray that God will lead you to those special adults. Set a time to
meet with that person. Present the challenge of the position. Let
him know *all* the responsibilities your church requires. Show the
prospective worker the materials he will need to accomplish his task
(curriculum, records, etc.). Be realistic about the job. Don't under-
rate it. Describe the training your church will provide before and
after he accepts. Ask the prospective worker to pray about all he has
heard. Make an appointment to come back next week for his
answer. Accept a "no" gracefully. Remember, you prayed for the
"right" person. Don't forget to follow up.

There are many adults in your church who like people, are
trainable, are maturing individuals, good team members and capa-
ble of leadership. Pray! You will find them.

*Starting or Maintaining Good Adult Workers' Meetings*

Adult Sunday School classes should be meaningful and alive!
This does not just happen. Planning needs to take place for effective
reaching, teaching, ministry and witnessing to result.

—A good planning meeting will help the adult worker get ready for
   Bible study sessions.

—It will help the worker plan how to involve members in the tasks of the Sunday School.

—Good planning will help the adult worker deal with administrative needs, evaluate training needs, determine specific plans for witnessing and ministering, develop a team spirit and establish the direction of the adult Sunday School.

All workers should attend planning meetings. However, if at least three-fourths of your workers attend on a regular basis, effective ministry can occur.

Planning meetings need to be worthwhile for workers. Everyone is busy. If workers' meetings do not meet the adult workers' need, they will not attend. The following suggestions for schedules might help:

(1) Have a general period lasting approximately 20 minutes for all adult workers. During this time have a prayer time, discuss administrative needs, and plan for reaching, witnessing and ministry. Use the remaining 40 minutes for each class to plan together for teaching and organizing the room, supplies and materials needed for Sunday morning.

(2) You may want to have a general meeting of all workers for 10 minutes and use the remaining 50 minutes in individual rooms, planning for reaching, witnessing, and ministering, setting up rooms, supplies and materials.

Don't forget to plan for social times together also. Team spirit is built through these much needed times of fellowship.

*Training Adult Workers*

Every adult worker needs to be thoroughly trained to perform his or her tasks in an efficient and productive manner. The tasks of reaching, teaching, witnessing and ministering are of utmost importance.

—Encourage your church to begin a potential workers' training program. Train workers before they begin teaching.

—Encourage your workers to attend clinics, seminars and conferences.

—Provide on-the-job training.

—Train in workers' meeting.
—Read books about the adult to whom you will minister.
—View videotapes, filmstrips and movies.
—Read lesson suggestions carefully.
—Practice skills learned.
—Study your Bible daily.
—Share training received with other adult workers.

Training can be fun.
—Train during a picnic.
—Train at a progressive dinner (summarize a chapter of a book at each course).
—Train during a breakfast or lunch.
Train to be the best adult worker possible.

*Evaluating Adult Space*

Most churches want to grow, but some churches do not understand that, in order to grow, new space must be provided. Educate your church! Help the members to know that overcrowded classes do not promote growth or ministry and to understand the benefits of finding new space.

Enlist the aid of all members in finding additional space. Get ideas from everyone. Don't let negatives destroy your mission. Evaluate present space. Remove items not needed or broken. Make whatever space you have attractive. Fix up. Paint. Put class signs and ages on doors. Rearrange furnishings occasionally. Don't be discouraged with inadequate facilities. Risk the new! Try the untried! Provide the space and adults will fill it.

## Your Adult Classes' Ministry Program

*Making Adult Contacts*

At least one-half of the adults enrolled in Sunday School need to be contacted each week. One-half? Yes, one-half. Think about that adult class that has twenty-five enrolled. Probably only ten to twelve attend on a regular basis. That's over one-half that do not attend. Certainly those adults need to be contacted.

What about those adults that attend regularly? They need to know you care about them. They need to be contacted too. Now, you have already exceeded one-half of your enrollment that need to be contacted. A growing adult class needs to contact at least one-half their enrollment each week.

Send cards. Write letters. Make phone calls. Go visiting. Contact adults in their homes or businesses.

*Adult Outreachers*

At least one adult worker from each adult class needs to visit each week.

Every adult needs a visit once in a while. That adult may need someone to listen as he talks about the trials of losing a job, a loved one or possessions. Adults need witnessing visits. Helping someone come to know Christ as his Savior is one of life's most rewarding experiences. Adults need ministry visits. Relationships are built as that adult worker helps someone move, paint, provide a meal or child-care during a crisis. Through these relationships witnessing takes place. Just imagine how strong your church will become when at least one person reaches out from each class each week!

## Your Adult Classes' Bible Teaching Program

*Adult Sunday School Attendance*

Adult Sunday School attendance needs to equal at least one-half the total enrollment. At least thirteen adults need to attend Sunday School from the class on the sample Spiral. How do you get at least one-half your enrollment to attend on a regular basis? Do the basics! Find prospects, enroll them, provide places for them to meet, have enough workers, provide time for those workers to plan, train the workers, make contacts and reach out. The people will come. Those adults will know you care. Something will be happening when they arrive. The workers will know what they are doing and they will do it well. The workers will be contacting and reaching out. No wonder adults will attend. Wouldn't you?

Adult workers cannot do what they are called by God to do if the people don't come. Take the time to do the right tasks, and you will have adults to teach, reach, witness to and minister to.

### Adult Worship Service Attendance

The number of adults in attendance in worship service is the same as for Sunday School—at least one-half your total enrollment.

More adults may attend the worship service than Sunday School classes in your church. If this is true try to enroll those adults in Sunday School. Sunday School members are more committed to the work of the church than those who only attend worship service. They will make better church members, as well as Sunday School members.

### Adult Offerings

Those adults who attend worship service only, give about 50 cents per capita as compared to those who attend Sunday School (who give about $20 per capita). Helping adults learn the biblical truths about tithing will benefit the adult, as well as the church.

### Adult Baptisms

Every adult worker should be involved in witnessing positively to non-Christians. Adult workers should create opportunities to witness. Adult workers should see witnessing as their primary task. When adults are discovered, enrolled, ministered to and contacted, this is only the beginning for the adult worker. Through that ministry, an opportunity for witnessing should take place. Adults will be baptized in your adult classes when adult workers witness verbally and through their actions.

Adult workers: use the Adult Sunday School Growth Spiral to be the best possible adult worker.

# 16
# The Youth Spiral

### Interpretation

Inside the back of this book you will find a completed Youth Sunday School Growth Spiral. Look at it, and follow it during the reading of this chapter.

### Quantity

Begin the Youth Spiral with the date of the quarter (10/1, 1/1, 4/1, 7/1) that is closest. The sample Spiral has been started with 10/1.

*Enrollment*

The present enrollment of a youth class (unit) is placed in this block. On the sample Spiral you will notice that the present enrollment in this unit is fifteen. The best size for a growing youth class is no more than ten, including the teacher. Therefore, I have placed a minus in this block. This youth class is too large for the best growth and ministry to take place. When you fill out your spiral, place a plus or minus here according to your enrollment.

Next, you need to set a yearly enrollment goal. Divide this yearly goal by four. A quarterly goal is much easier to reach and work toward when it is broken down into a manageable time frame. Fill in the remaining blocks on the Spiral with the quarterly enrollment goals.

You will notice that an enrollment goal of two youth per quarter has been placed on the sample Spiral. Now, the enrollment goal for

1/1 is 17, 4/1 is 19, 7/1 is 21, and by 10/1 of next year, the goal will be 23 youth enrolled.

Note: When you actually reach the maximum recommended enrollment goal for a unit (ten including the teacher) you would start a new unit. Then, you would make out new Spirals for the two classes. Since this is a teaching Spiral, not an actual youth class, I will complete the year on one Spiral as an example.

*Prospects:*

The current number of youth prospects with name, address, phone number and age is placed in this first block. On the sample Spiral there are eight prospects for this class. I have placed a minus under this column also because you will need to have at least the same number of prospects as you have youth enrolled in order to have enough prospects for your class to continue to grow. One of the primary reasons for nongrowth is the lack of valid prospects.

## Quality

*Teaching Units*

If you are filling out a Spiral for your own class (unit), place a 1 in this column as I have on the sample Spiral, because this Spiral is for one class or unit.

Moving up the Spiral, divide the enrollment by 10 (maximum recommended enrollment including teacher) and that will give you the number of units needed. On the sample Spiral you will notice that two units are needed by 1/1. No new units need to be added by 4/1, but by 7/1 a third unit should be.

A minus has been placed under the Units column on the sample Spiral because there are fifteen youth enrolled in one unit on 10/1, which exceeds the maximum recommended enrollment of ten, including teacher.

*Workers*

Each new class needs at least two workers—a teacher and a youth to serve as class leader. On the sample Spiral there are three teachers for this class—thus, a plus. If you have enough teachers for your unit when you fill out your Spiral, give yourself a plus here.

*Workers' Meeting*

Youth workers need a time to come together to administer and plan for Bible study, outreach, witnessing and ministry. They *need* to attend workers' meetings. All three of the workers in the youth class on the sample Spiral attend workers' meetings on a regular basis, so a plus has been placed under this column.

At least three-fourths of the workers in a youth unit need to be in attendance at workers' meetings to earn a plus. Youth workers teach and minister on a weekly basis and should plan on a weekly basis. Three-fourths of 3 is 2.25. Therefore, three teachers need to be present.

*Training Awards*

One of the keys to successful and effective teaching, reaching, witnessing and ministry is consistent training. Train yourself to be the best youth worker you can be. You may receive training awards for any book you read, or class, seminar or conference you attend that will help you minister to youth.

Training awards must equal at least one-half the number of workers in order to rate a plus. On the sample Spiral zero training awards were earned last quarter, thus, a minus under this column. In order to get a plus this class needed two training awards last quarter (three months).

## Outreach/Ministry

*Space*

Place the number of spaces available for youth classes in this block. Hopefully, there will be a space for every youth class needed.

*Contacts*

Contacts (cards, letters, phone calls, visits) need to be made weekly. This and the Outreachers columns are the only weekly goals on the Spiral. Youth workers cannot wait three months to make contacts and visit—hence, weekly goals.

On the sample Spiral notice that eight contacts were made last week. In order to place a plus here, contacts should equal at least one-half the enrollment. Fifteen are enrolled on 10/1; eight contacts were made last week, a plus. Remember, as the enrollment increases contacts need to increase.

## Outreachers

Outreachers are those youth workers who visit. The number of cards, letters, phone calls or visits do not count here. People count here. How many are out visiting each week from each class? The goal is for one worker from each class (unit) to visit each week. On the sample Spiral there is a plus because one of the workers from this class visited last week.

## Projections

### Sunday School Attendance

The current average Sunday School attendance goes in this first block. This number includes workers and youth enrolled in each class. A plus has been placed in this column because at least one-half of the enrollment attended on the average this quarter. As the enrollment increases the number in attendance at Sunday School should increase.

### Worship Service Attendance

Place the average worship service attendance per quarter for your class in this block. On the sample Spiral an average of eight attend worship service also. A plus has been placed in this column, too, because at least one-half the enrollment is in attendance on an average.

### Offerings

Current offerings per quarter are placed in this block. If you want to know the per capita giving for your class, divide the offerings by the Sunday School attendance.

### Baptisms

Place the number of baptisms that came from your class last quarter here. Place the number of baptisms you would like to have from your class each quarter in the succeeding blocks as you work your way up the Spiral.

Youth workers: use the Youth Sunday School Growth Spiral to reach, teach, witness and minister to your youth more effectively.

## Implementation

## Your Youth Classes' Outreach Ministry

*Finding and Enrolling Youth Prospects*

Youth workers will reach more youth when they plan and organize for outreach. Finding and enrolling youth does not just happen. Youth workers should commit themselves to finding and enrolling youth—and then organize to do so.

They should continue to discover more prospects. Youth classes will not grow without prospects. Begin or update a prospect file. In this file make sure each prospect is listed by name, address, phone number and age. Class leaders are responsible for contacting and ministering to each prospect.

Youth workers should involve youth in reaching other youth. After all, this is their peer group, and they have constant contact with other youth.

Use every training resource you can find to help you reach out more effectively. Read books. Attend classes, seminars and conferences.

Visit and contact youth regularly. Enroll youth anytime, anyplace, as long as they consent. Don't wait for them to attend three times. Enroll them now. When a youth is enrolled, someone becomes responsible to minister to him or her. Stay in touch with the youth who are already enrolled. They also need to be contacted and ministered to.

Look for youth prospects at social events, theaters, malls, ball games and other sporting events. Encourage youth at school to invite schoolmates to revivals, retreats, camps, churchwide fellowships, Sunday School, worship service or Bible study.

Youth are everywhere. Find them, invite them, contact them, minister to them and *enroll* them. Remember, an aggressive enrollment emphasis is needed to reach a maximum number of prospects.

## Your Youth Classes' Organizational Program

*Finding Additional Youth Space*

Every growing church has a problem finding all the rooms it needs. Finding additional space and keeping the numbers in the classes small is vital to ministry, outreach, enrollment and witnessing. Youth need the personal attention small classes allow. Caring youth Bible study occurs when the youth teacher and the students form a good relationship. Personal attention and the one-on-one relationship decreases as the enrollment increases.

When looking for youth classes, consider the age, school grade and gender of the youth. Twelve-year-olds and seventeen-year-olds have different needs. Consider starting new classes to separate ages. You may choose to form classes based on school grades. Start coed classes if this is appropriate for the youth at your church.

When you reach out to unenrolled youth, think about the class they will attend. Is it overcrowded? The visiting youth may feel awkward, unwelcome, lost in the crowd, and not feel like part of the group.

—Walk through your church looking for new places in which to meet. See if there are any rooms not being used that would be suitable. All youth classes do not have to be in the same area.
—What about the choir loft, the sanctuary, foyer, choir room, prayer room, fellowship hall, vans, buses or RV's?
—Look around your community. Try to stay within a one-mile radius of your church. Are there any schools, businesses or homes that could provide more space?

Youth Sunday School classes should always be growing. Keep classes small to effectively reach, witness, minister, and win as many youth as possible.

## Your Youth Classes' Discipleship Ministry

*Finding Youth Workers*

—A good youth worker is someone who has a sound relationship with God, himself, youth and other youth workers.

—A good youth worker is a listener, a witness, a minister, a teacher, an instructor, a guide, a facilitator, a leader, a learner and an example.

—A good youth worker understands the youth he teaches and truly cares for youth. Just knowing about the Bible is not enough for a good youth worker. Through genuine concern for youth, that worker can create an interest in God's truths. He can lead youth to become excited about spiritual growth.

Your church may already have procedures for finding youth workers. If so, follow those. If not:

—Involve the entire church in finding good youth workers.
—Enlist youth workers personally.
—Make an appointment to talk to the person selected.
—Share written responsibilities with the prospective worker.
—Emphasize the importance of the task.
—Encourage your church to participate in a potential leadership training program.
—Potential workers can attend classes to explore the possibility of working with youth.

Youth workers are everywhere in your church. Pray that God will lead you to the right persons.

## Youth Workers' Meeting

At least three-fourths of your youth workers need to be in workers' meetings on a regular basis so your teaching, reaching, ministry and witnessing will be effective. Exciting, life-changing Bible study needs to take place on Sunday morning. That does not happen without planning.

—Administrative needs of your youth class need to be discussed.
—Workers need to discuss how to involve youth in accomplishing the task of the Sunday School.
—Specific plans need to be made for witnessing and outreach.
—Concerns, successes, and opportunities need to be discussed.
—Fellowships need to be planned.

—Prayer, team spirit and an awareness of the presence of the Holy Spirit needs to take place.

Workers' meetings must have the commitment of the church, priority scheduling, high expectations and positive results in order to be successful. Something positive must happen!

(1) Schedule your workers' meeting so there is a 20-minute general period where all workers meet together. During this time, prayer, administering class concerns, and planning for reaching, witnessing and ministering occur. The remaining 40 minutes may be used for planning for teaching and learning.

(2) You may choose to spend 15 minutes together in the entire youth area where youth concerns are discussed. A general period lasting 5 minutes may follow, with the remaining 40 minutes used for class concerns such as reaching, witnessing, ministering and planning for teaching and learning.

(3) A third schedule suggestion would be for a 10-minute general period with all workers together. The remaining 50 minutes could be used for planning. Choose a schedule that best suits your needs. The most important consideration is that you *plan to plan*. Planning is an ongoing process because youth ministry, reaching, teaching and witnessing are ongoing processes. Plan to be the best youth worker possible.

*Training Youth Workers*

Youth workers need to be trained. Youth classes can create an environment for training by stressing training during the enlistment process. Tell those prospective youth workers they will be trained, and that they are expected to attend training events. Encourage your church to place a high priority on training.

—Promote training events regularly.
—Keep abreast with training events happening nearby.
—Keep a training calendar.
—Ask your church to budget for training events.
—Identify the training wants and needs of youth workers.
—Maintain a record of training experiences and accomplishments of youth workers.

—Recognize the training accomplishments of youth workers.
—Conduct potential workers' training classes.
—Begin on-the-job training.
—Train in workers' meetings.
—Attend clinics, conferences and classes.
—Read books about youth.
—Use videotapes and other audiovisuals.
—Provide personal learning activities.

Training should be available to meet the needs of all youth workers. Since not all workers can attend training at the same time, vary the training events.

—Meet on Saturday or Sunday morning.
—Try Friday night and Saturday or all day Sunday.
—Meet one day/night for several weeks.
—Try two days/nights for several weeks.
—Maybe one night a week for several weeks with a covered-dish supper.
—Or, a Sunday afternoon with lunch provided.

Trained youth workers can more effectively influence youth toward a greater involvement in discovering and applying Bible truths. Training is essential.

*Evaluating Youth Space*

Help your church understand that new classes will reach more youth. Begin those new classes when the church year begins. Motivation and excitement are high at this time.

Start new classes when old classes reach maximum recommended enrollment of ten. Start new classes anytime there is a need.

Constantly evaluate the learning environment.

—Use as few furnishings and equipment as possible.
—Remove all clutter.
—Vary the room arrangements occasionally.
—Do not be discouraged by inadequate facilities.
—Focus on the central truth for the session.

—Don't be afraid to risk the new and untried.
—Youth can learn in any environment with a committed and creative teacher.

### Your Youth Classes' Ministry Program

*Contacting Youth*

A growing Sunday School must contact at least one-half of their
enrollment each week. Youth need to know you care for them and
virtually cry out for you to show your concern. Youth need to know
they are accepted and part of the group. Youth will bring their
friends to a place they enjoy. Make that place your Sunday School.

Contact youth through phone calls, cards and letters. Have social
events that youth want to attend. Visit youth in their homes. Contact youth at sporting events, malls, businesses, playgrounds—any
place lost youth may be.

—Contact youth to witness to them.
—Contact youth to minister to them.
—Contact youth to reach out to them, to show them concern and
love.
—Contact youth to enroll them in Bible study.
—Contact youth to meet their needs.

*Youth Outreachers*

At least one youth worker from each youth class needs to visit
each week.

—Visit the youth who has an unhappy home life. Be the listener he
needs.
—Visit the youth who is lost and does not know where to turn. Be
the witness he needs.
—Visit the youth who needs someone to support him. Be the friend
he needs.
—Visit the youth who needs a positive influence in his life. Be the
Sunday School class he needs.

There are as many reasons to visit as there are youth with needs.
Through the relationships built when visiting, the youth worker can

share those experiences and Bible truths that can change the life of that youth forever. Visit, visit, visit.

## Your Youth Classes' Bible Teaching Program

*Youth Sunday School Attendance*

When the youth worker finds and enrolls youth, has enough prospects, has enough room for those enrolled, has enough workers for those youth enrolled, attends workers' meetings to plan for teaching, witnessing, reaching and ministry, is trained, makes contacts and reaches out—youth will attend. That is the reason behind doing these actions.

—If youth attend, they can participate in Bible-related activities.
—They will be witnessed to.
—They will be ministered to.
—They will be surrounded by Christian peers and influences.
—The youth worker is better able to witness, minister, teach and reach.

*Youth Worship Attendance*

Worship service attendance is important for youth also. Youth need to feel a part of the entire church as well as a class.

Involve youth in the worship service for better attendance.

Youth can:
—Usher.
—Serve as assistant pastor or camera operator.
—Be a custodian.
—Write or print church newsletters or bulletins.
—Participate in music program.
—Be a worshiper.

*Youth Offerings*

Helping youth develop the habit of tithing will benefit the youth as well as the church. Keeping a chart showing the amount of offerings collected in each class emphasizes this teaching.

*Youth Baptisms*

Each youth worker should see the sharing of God's salvation as a basic joy and privilege. Through the relationships developed, the Bible truths taught, and the Christian experiences shared, the youth worker should embark youth on a Christian pilgrimage by helping them grow as Christians, and eventually share their faith with others. This is the priority of youth Sunday School.

# 17

# The Children's Spiral

## Interpretation

The Children's Growth Spiral can be made out for individual rooms or for the entire division (all the rooms).

The ratio chart below will help as you work with the Spiral for children, grades one through six.

| CHILDREN'S DIVISION | | | |
|---|---|---|---|
| | *Teacher-Pupil Ratio* | *Maximum Department Enrollment* | *Square Feet Needed Per Person* |
| Children (Grades 1-6) | 1 worker to 7 children | 30 Pupils and workers | Minimum 20 Square Feet Recommended 25 Square Feet |

Inside the back of the book you will find a completed Children's Sunday School Growth Spiral. Follow it during the reading of this chapter.

This is a sample teaching Spiral for a children's room (grades 1-6), not an actual children's room.

## Quantity

*Date*

Begin with the Date column. You will notice on the sample Spiral that I have placed the date of the beginning of the church year—10/1 (October 1). You may begin with the date of the quarter closest when you begin filling out your spiral (10/1, 1/1, 4/1, 7/1). Above this date, the year is divided into four quarters—1/1, 4/1, 7/1, and back to 10/1. It is easier to reach a quarterly goal than an annual goal.

*Enrollment*

Begin with your present enrollment, then divide the enrollment into how many are teachers and how many are children. This will be different than if you were filling out a church Spiral because of the teacher/pupil ratio (1 to 7).

On the sample Spiral the total enrollment is twenty-four. Twenty-one are children (grades 1-6) and three are teachers (21/24/3). Later, when you develop your own Spiral, you will place your room or division's enrollment in this location.

Three teachers for twenty-one children enrolled is the correct ratio (1 to 7) so notice the plus ( + ) under Enrollment on the sample Spiral. The maximum enrollment for a children's room is thirty, so twenty-four does not exceed the correct ratio. When you fill out your Spiral, if you do not have the proper ratio of teachers and children or exceed the maximum enrollment per room (30), put a minus (-) under Enrollment.

A plus or a minus is a simple evaluation tool. It is valuable in helping you see the strengths and weaknesses in your room or division. This evaluation tool lets you know if you are growing, maintaining or declining. This is the primary reason for starting the Spiral with the Enrollment column.

On the sample Spiral a goal has been set to enroll two children each quarter or eight a year. You may decide to enroll more or less children each quarter.

Since there are already twenty-one children enrolled at the beginning of the sample Spiral, there will be twenty-three children enrolled by 1/1. Therefore, one new teacher will need to be added to keep the teacher/pupil ratio of one to seven. The block for 1/1 should now be 23/27/4. By 4/1 we should have twenty-five children enrolled and four teachers for a total enrollment of twenty-nine (25/29/4). By 7/1, twenty-seven children and four teachers (27/31/4), and by 10/1, twenty-nine children and five teachers (29/34/5). Later, in this chapter, you will see how to increase the enrollment to meet your goals.

*Note:* When you actually reach the maximum enrollment capacity for a room (30) you would start a new room and a new Spiral for both. Since this is a teaching Spiral, however, I will complete the year on one Spiral as an example.

## Prospects

The next column is labeled Prospects. Notice on the sample Spiral that there are five prospects. When you fill out your Spiral you will put the number of the prospects you have at the present time for your room or division. A valid prospect is a child, grades one to six, that you have the name, address and, hopefully, the phone number for. The number of prospects entered should equal at least the number of children you have enrolled in your room or division. Therefore, I have placed a minus on the sample Spiral under the Prospects column because I have twenty-one children enrolled and only five prospects at this time. One of the primary reasons for nongrowth is a lack of valid prospects.

## Quality

### Teaching Units

In the children's area we call a teaching unit a room or department. In the adult and youth area we call a teaching unit a class. Because of the different terminology for the various age groups we will call a class, room or department a teaching unit.

The recommended maximum enrollment, not attendance, for a children's room is thirty. Because children's teachers are required to do much more than teach, this maximum is important. A children's teacher must reach out, minister, witness and plan, as well as teach.

When the enrollment exceeds thirty, all these ministries begin to decline and perhaps even stop taking place.

As an example, think of yourself as a teacher of third-grade students. The teachers in your room are doing a great job of reaching out, ministering, witnessing, planning and teaching. Your room has grown rapidly this year. You now have thirty-five third-grade students in your room. Are you and your teachers really going out to find more third graders? The chances are that you are struggling to maintain with the ones you already have. Now, your outreach has stopped. Are you able to visit as often as when you had fewer students? Your witnessing has now declined. How about your ability to give those children individual attention as you teach? Can't get around to all of them as you would like? Your teaching has declined.

Starting new children's teaching units is imperative for quality teaching, reaching, ministering and witnessing. What do you think would happen if you started a new teaching unit from that room with thirty-five third graders? This would be two classes with seventeen and eighteen children, respectively. Do you think your ministry, witnessing, teaching and outreach would improve? I think so too.

On the sample Spiral there is a total enrollment of twenty-four (teachers and children). This is within the recommended maximum enrollment of thirty so I have placed a plus under the Units column.

When you fill out your Spiral and begin your evaluation, don't be discouraged if you are getting some minuses. Those minuses will show you at a glance the areas of weakness in your room and ministry, and *that's* a plus!

*Workers*

In the children's area a worker is another name for a teacher. We count only those workers (teachers) who are enrolled and teaching when we fill out a Spiral for a children's room or division. This is different than when a Spiral is filled out for the entire church. But, if others than those who are teaching are counted, the teacher/pupil ratio (1 to 7) is thrown off in a children's room or division.

On the sample Spiral you will see there are three teachers for twenty-one children, so there is a plus under the Workers column. Place a plus or minus under that column when you fill out your Spiral according to how many teachers you have per child. Remember, as you move up the Spiral and increase your enrollment to meet your quarterly goals, you must also increase the number of teachers.

*Workers' Meeting*

On the sample Spiral, two of the three teachers in this room attend workers' meetings on a regular basis. I have placed a minus under this column because three-fourths of your teachers need to be in attendance at workers' meetings to plan effectively for what will be taught on Sunday morning. Three-fourths of 3 is 2.25. Therefore, when you have three teachers in a room all three must attend on a regular basis. The more teachers you have in a room, the fewer will have to attend in order to have three-fourths there.

Evaluate your room or division and add a plus or minus. Then, project how many teachers you will need in attendance as you progress quarter by quarter up the Spiral.

Now you are beginning to see how to plan for the quality ministry you want, *and* you have goals to work toward in all areas of your ministry.

*Training Awards*

Training awards are books you read, classes, seminars and conferences you attend to help you better teach, reach, witness and minister to children. Count anything you do that helps you become better prepared.

In order to gain a plus in this column, you must have training awards to equal at least one-half the number of workers, each quarter. For example: If you have four workers (teachers), you must have at least two training awards each quarters.

On the sample Spiral this room had no training awards last quarter, thus, a minus in this column. Remember, as you progress up the Spiral and add more teachers you must also add more training awards. Teachers *must* be trained and keep on training if they are to be effective in helping the children to accept Christ as their Savior and Lord and grow in the Christian faith.

## Outreach/Ministry

*Space*

Each person enrolled in a children's room needs at least 20 square feet of space. However, it is recommended that a children's room have 25 square feet per person enrolled (children and teachers).

On the sample Spiral there are twenty-four people enrolled in the room on 10/1. Therefore, that room needs to be at least 480 square feet and preferably 600 square feet. Rooms that are too small do not allow for growth nor do they lend themselves to teaching the child properly. Try to start out with a room that will allow for at least thirty enrolled (the maximum recommended). If the room is not large enough for thirty, start another unit when it reaches its maximum.

*Contacts*

The number of contacts made each week in a children's room should equal at least one-half the number of children enrolled. Past records will probably indicate that only one-half of the children enrolled in a room or division are attending on a given Sunday. At the very least those children need to be contacted.

On the sample Spiral, I have placed a minus because only three contacts were made last week. This and the Outreachers columns are the only columns that are counted on a weekly basis. You cannot wait three months (a quarter) to contact your children. You must contact them on a weekly basis. On the sample Spiral there are twenty-one children enrolled, so eleven contacts must be made each week for a plus to be placed in this column. As the number of children enrolled increases, the number of weekly contacts should increase.

*Outreachers*

Outreachers are those teachers who make visits. Cards, phone calls and letters are not counted in the Outreachers column. In order to get a plus, at least one teacher from each room each week needs to be making visits. There are three teachers on the sample spiral on 10/1, but that is for one room. Therefore, only one teacher visiting per week will be a plus. In this room no one visited last week, so a minus was placed in this column.

Can you imagine what happens to an entire church when all the teaching units have at least one person visiting each week?

## Projections

*Sunday School Attendance*

Place the average Sunday School attendance this quarter for your room or division in the first block under Sunday School Attendance. On the sample Spiral, thirteen of the twenty-one children enrolled attend Sunday School on an average for the quarter. I have placed a plus in this column because at least one-half of the total enrollment (teachers and children) were in attendance. There are twenty-four enrolled and thirteen attended, a plus.

*Worship Service Attendance*

Attendance in the Worship Service Attendance column should be the teachers and children who go to the worship service or stay for children's worship, or whatever your church provides.

Place a plus or minus here if the attendance is at least one-half of the Sunday enrollment. There are twenty-four people enrolled, and at least twelve must be in attendance. A plus is placed here because thirteen attend on an average each quarter.

A plus was placed in both the Sunday School and the Worship Attendance columns. But, thirteen out of a total enrollment of twenty-four is barely one-half the total enrollment. What about those other eleven children enrolled who do not attend?

Study the sample Spiral, and you will find your answer. The room is not overcrowded and there are enough teachers. But not enough of those teachers are in planning meeting each week, planning for Sunday morning. The teachers are getting little or no training. They do not make enough contacts each week, and they do not visit on a weekly basis. I am surprised that attendance is as high as it is.

—The children *must* know that you love and care for them.
—You *must* be trained, and you must be well prepared.
—You *must* reach out and witness.
Then, the children will come.

You may be the best children's teacher in the church, but if the children do not attend, you can't teach them. Use the Children's Sunday School Growth Spiral to help you be the best teacher God has called you to be.

## Implementation

### Your Children's Room or Division Outreach Ministry

*Enrolling and Finding Children's Prospects*

The tasks of the children's teacher are important and varied. Children's teachers need to be prepared:

—To witness to families of children not enrolled in Sunday School.
—To show they are concerned for children not enrolled in Sunday School.
—To seek out children not enrolled in Sunday School.
—To lead the parents of children to Christ.
—To help children and their families see the need to participate in Bible study through the Sunday School.
—To share with children the biblical message of God's plan of redemption.

In order to be able to accomplish these tasks, children's teachers must find those children and their families. How do you find children prospects? Check some of the ideas you may want to try listed below:

———— List unchurched children from Vacation Bible School.
———— Identify homes where children are playing outside.
———— Ask youth to survey the block where they live.
———— Look on the block where you live.
———— Subscribe to newcomer services.
———— Ask neighborhood ice cream vendors.
———— Confer with military base chaplains.

———— Follow up on Sunday School guests (visitors).
———— Follow up on worship service guests (visitors).
———— Ask bus ministry riders to identify other children on their route.
———— Follow up on families reached through bus ministry.
———— Provide social events for parents without partners.
———— Request information on prospects from baby sitters.
———— Provide a Parent's Night Out.
———— "I Know a Children's Prospect" cards.

These are a few suggestions you may want to try. There are many other ways to find unenrolled children and their families. Meet with the other teachers of children. Discuss together ways they think will work.

Take time to evaluate what you are already doing in your children's room.

---

*Finding and Enrolling Children Prospects*

1. It's OK to enroll children after their first visit.
   ———— (a) Yes
   ———— (b) No
2. I look for children prospects on a regular basis.
   ———— (a) Yes
   ———— (b) No
3. I follow up on those children who visit in my room and try to enroll them in Sunday School.
   ———— (a) Yes
   ———— (b) No
4. I enroll children anytime, anyplace, if they or their parents give consent.
   ———— (a) Yes
   ———— (b) No

---

Give yourself 10 points for every yes answer and 5 points for every no answer.

40 GOOD JOB!
30 NEEDS IMPROVEMENT.
20 TRY HARDER!

Unless they attend you cannot share the Word of God with them. Go find them, invite them to come and meet their needs. They will continue to come back when they know you love and care for them. From the relationship you build with the children and their families, you will be able to share your own Christian experience and perhaps lead them to make a life commitment to Christ.

## Your Children's Room or Division
## Organizational Program

*Finding Additional Children Rooms*

The entire church cannot grow in balance unless every area of the church grows. Therefore, every age group needs additional space, not just adults. Finding additional space for adults is important, but if a church does not find additional space for children also, the adults who bring children will not come back when their child's room is too crowded.

Additional space is hard to find in a growing church. All age groups need to meet together to find additional space for one another. Preschoolers and senior adults need space on the ground level. They cannot manipulate stairs as well as other ages. Adults and youth can meet in some unusual places to make room for children who are less flexible.

Remember, try to keep each group of children to a maximum enrollment of thirty. Ministry, witnessing, as well as teaching, takes place in a children's room. When too many children are in a room you will find all areas of your ministry will decline or even cease. Depending on the number of children you have in your church, you may want to have one or more rooms for each grade (1-6). If you have only enough children for two rooms you may want to place grades one to three in one room and grades four to six in the other. In three rooms you might place grades 1-2, 3-4 and 5-6 together. Arrange rooms according to how many children you have enrolled, not by how many rooms you have. *Find* additional space if needed.

If your church is truly committed to grow, you will find additional space. See the preschool chapter for suggestions. Some additional suggestions are:

—Meet in the church library.
—Try various parts of the sanctuary if a pastor's class is not being held.
—Look for a school nearby.
—Does a church member have a home nearby?
—Section off a large room to make two or more rooms.
—Meet outside in nice weather.
—Give or throw away items not needed or used.
—Suggest another meeting place for youth or adults (they're more flexible) to free up a room for children.

When you are looking for additional space, try to allow 25 square feet per person enrolled.

## Your Children's Room or Division Discipleship Ministry

*Finding Children's Workers*

Workers (teachers) with children, as with all age groups, are special people. They should have a personal relationship with the Lord, continue to grow in the Lord, have a concern for children, be willing to plan and train, be dependable, be willing to change, support the church, know (or will learn) about the child they teach and be able to cooperate with others.

Review the chapter about how to enlist preschool teachers for suggestions about enlisting a children's teacher. Basically, the method is the same. Pray for the right person. Make an appointment to see that person. Let the person know *all* his responsibilities in advance. Ask him to pray about it. Make an appointment to return for his answer in a week. Accept a yes or no answer.

Try to have one teacher for seven children, and remember, you are looking for committed Christian teachers.

*Children's Workers' Meeting*

One of the responsibilities the potential teacher should recognize in advance is the need to attend weekly workers' meetings. Teaching is done weekly, so planning should be done weekly.

Have a well-planned, thought-out workers' meeting. Teachers are busy people. Dedicated as they are, they will not continue to attend a meeting that does not speak to them or help them plan for Sunday.

Plan a schedule and stick to it as closely as possible. Set a time limit for each item on your agenda. A suggested schedule might be: Inspiration—5 minutes; administration—5 minutes; reaching and ministry—10 minutes; training—10 minutes; planning—30 minutes.

Workers' meetings are for interpretation, previewing, understanding, growth, fellowship, training, reviewing, praying, planning, asking, helping, assigning, doing, study, promoting, motivation, learning, inspiring, sharing and recognizing. Take turns assigning teachers the responsibility for each week's inspiration and training. Let everyone feel a part of each meeting. Promote planning and workers' meeting attendance. Try to have at least three-fourths of your teachers attend on a regular basis. If you don't plan for Sunday morning, chances are the children will plan it for you!

*Training Children's Workers*
—Because the children's teacher will need to teach children grades 1-6, train to understand the child you teach.
—Because children's teachers will need to witness to parents and children, train to know how to witness.
—Because you will need to teach Bible-related activities, train to know how to teach effectively.
—Train to know how to set up a children's room for optimum teaching.
—Train to minister, contact, visit.

Where can you get training?

—Ask your pastor what training events are planned in your church and in your immediate area. Usually this training is free.

—Call some of the other churches in your area. See if they know of any training events that are planned.

—Watch for listings in the newspaper for training events.

—Ask other teachers.

Train to be the best teacher you can be. Remember, you need training awards each quarter to equal at least one-half the number of teachers in your room.

## Evaluating Children's Space

The minimum amount of space to plan for in a children's room is 20 square feet per person enrolled. It is recommended that you try to have 25 square feet per person enrolled.

Begin with a room that is large enough for the maximum recommended enrollment of thirty. As you reach out and grow, hopefully you will reach that goal, and you will need a room large enough. At 25 square feet per person enrolled you will need a room that is 750 square feet.

## Your Children's Room or Division
## Ministry Program

*Contacting Children*

—Contact those children who are absent.

—Contact those who attend all the time. They also like to know you care.

—Contact those who visit your room.

—Contact children on their birthday.

—Contact to meet a special need.

—Contact any prospects you find.

—Contact to build relationships.

—Contact to enroll.

—Contact to share your testimony.

—Contact to be a friend.

On the sample Spiral, under the Contacts column, there is a minus because not enough contacts were made each week.

*Children's Outreachers*

Outreachers are those who go out and visit. One person from every children's room should be visiting each week. Cards, phone calls and letters are not counted here. Those who visit are Outreachers.

Here are some ways to be an outreacher:

—Take a child to a doctor's appointment for working parents.
—Child-sit while parents run errands.
—Invite children to play in your yard if they don't have one.
—Take a meal to a newcomer.
—Grocery shop for a sick parent.
—Teach a motherless child simple skills.
—Call a discouraged parent and tell him or her you will pray for him.
—Listen, listen, listen.
—Help a child through a death in the family.
—Let a child from a broken home know he is loved.
—Help a jobless parent find work.
—Best of all, you may want to visit to help a parent or child know Christ as his or her Savior.

## Your Children's Division's Bible Teaching Program

*Children's Sunday School Attendance*

On an average at least one-half of your total enrollment (children and teachers) should be in attendance.

When you have enough teachers, do not exceed the maximum total enrollment (30). Train, attend workers' meetings and plan. Have enough space, contact and reach out, and the children will come. When they come you can share Christ's love with them. Isn't that what God called you, as a children's teacher, to do?

*Children's Worship Attendance*

Count the teachers and children who attend worship service, stay for children's worship or whatever your church provides for children during this time. Do at least one-half of your total enrollment (teachers and children) attend? When you reach out and minister with love and concern, children will attend.

## Children's Offerings

Place the amount of the offering you had for the last quarter in the first block. Keep track of offerings each quarter and enter them in successive blocks. You may want to divide the amount received by the number of people you have in attendance to see what the per capita is. This will allow you to project the approximate amount you will receive each quarter in the future.

## Children's Baptisms

Place the number of baptisms you had from your room or division last quarter in the first block. Keep track of the number each successive quarter.

Children's teachers: You will be sharing your testimony with children and their families every time you show God's love and concern for them. Never forget how special you are.

# 18

# The Preschool Spiral

## Interpretation

The Preschool Growth Spiral can be filled out in several ways. You may choose to fill out a Spiral for your entire preschool division (all your preschool rooms). You may want to fill out a Spiral for babies through ones, twos and threes, fours and fives, or each individual room. Whichever grouping you choose, the principles will be the same—only the ratios will be different.

The ratio chart below will help you as you work with whatever age grouping you choose:

| PRESCHOOL DIVISION | | | | | |
| --- | --- | --- | --- | --- | --- |
| Age | Teacher-Pupil Ratio | Maximum Department Enrollment | | | Square Feet Needed Per Person Enrolled |
| | | Pre | Tea. | Total | |
| Babies-Ones | 1 to 3 | 9 | 3 | 12 | Minimum 20 Recommended 35 |
| Two-Year-Olds | 1 to 4 | 12 | 3 | 15 | Minimum 20 Recommended 35 |
| Three to Five-Year-Olds | 1 to 4 | 16 | 4 | 20 | Minimum 20 Recommended 35 |

Remember: Because pupil-teacher ratios are different for the different age groupings, statistics will be different for these age groupings. Use pupil-teacher ratios under Two-Year-Olds if you are filling out the Spiral for the entire preschool division (all the preschool rooms).

In the back of the book you will find a completed Preschool Sunday School Growth Spiral. Follow it during the reading of this chapter. This is a sample Spiral for a three- to five-year room, a teaching Spiral, not an actual room.

## Quantity

*Date*

First, there is the Date column. You will notice in the first block I have placed the date of the beginning of the church year—10/1 (October 1). You may begin with the date of the quarter closest when you begin filling out your spiral (10/1, 1/1, 4/1, 7/1). Above this date, the year is divided into four quarters—1/1, 4/1, 7/1, and back to 10/1. It is easier to reach a quarterly goal than an annual goal.

*Enrollment*

Begin with your present enrollment, then divide the enrollment into how many are teachers and how many enrolled are preschoolers. This will be different from what you would do if you were filling out a church Spiral of the teacher-pupil ratios.

Notice that the total enrollment is twenty. Sixteen are three-year-olds, and four are teachers (16/20/4). Later, when you develop your own Spiral you will place your room or division's enrollment in this location. Four teachers for sixteen three-year-olds is a correct ratio (one-fourth) so notice the plus under Enrollment on the sample Spiral.

The maximum enrollment for one three-year-old room is twenty, so that is also a correct ratio. When you fill out your Spiral, if you do not have the proper ratio of teachers per pupil or exceed the maximum enrollment per room as previously indicated on the chart for your age group put a minus under Enrollment.

A plus or a minus is a simple evaluation tool, but it is valuable since it helps us see where our strengths and weaknesses are. Are we growing, maintaining or declining? This is the primary reason for starting our Spiral with the Enrollment column.

In order to fill out the other blocks in this segment of the Spiral, each department (room) or division must set a goal of how many preschoolers they wish to enroll for each quarter. If a yearly goal is set, it must then be divided into quarters.

On the sample Spiral a goal has been set of four preschoolers enrolled per quarter or sixteen per year. You may decide on a smaller or larger goal.

Since there are already sixteen preschoolers enrolled at the beginning of the sample Spiral there will be twenty preschoolers enrolled by 1/1. Therefore, one new teacher will need to be added to keep our teacher/pupil ratio of one to four. The block for 1/1 should now be 20/25/5. By 4/1 we should have twenty-four preschoolers enrolled and six teachers for a total enrollment of thirty (24/30/6). By 7/1, twenty-eight preschoolers enrolled and seven teachers for a total enrollment of thirty-five (28/35/7), and so on. Later, we will see how to increase the enrollment during the year to meet the goals you have set.

*Note:* When you actually reach the maximum enrollment capacity for a room, you would start a new room and a new Spiral for both of those rooms. Since this is a teaching Spiral, however, I will complete the year on one Spiral as an example.

*Prospects*

The next column is labeled Prospects. Notice that there are six prospects at this time on the sample Spiral. Prospects are those preschoolers for whom you have the names, addresses and, hopefully, phone numbers. The number of prospects entered should at least equal the number of preschoolers you have enrolled in your room or division. I have placed a minus under the Prospects column on the sample Spiral because there should be at least sixteen prospects at this time.

When you complete your Spiral, if the number of prospects equals or exceeds the number of preschoolers you have enrolled, place a plus under the Prospects column. Surveys have shown that we need at least as many prospects for enrollment as we have preschoolers who are enrolled. One of the primary reasons for nongrowth is a lack of valid prospects.

## Quality

*Teaching Units*

In the preschool area we call a teaching unit a room or department. In the adult and youth area we call a teaching unit a class. Because of the different terminology for the various age groups we will call a class, room or department a teaching unit.

On the chart in this chapter, observe that the maximum enrollment, not attendance, for babies through one-year-olds is twelve. For two-year-olds it is fifteen, and for three- through five-year-olds it is twenty. Because a preschool teacher is called to do much more than just teach on Sunday morning, these figures are extremely important.

Any teacher of babies through ones will tell you that when one baby cries the rest of them do too. When a teacher has to spend most of his or her time meeting needs (changing diapers, feeding, rocking, quieting) that teacher has little time actually to teach that baby about God on his level of understanding. (Can a baby learn about God? That is another book, and there are many already written that will help you understand that this is so.)

Because the younger the child, the more dependent he is, the fewer distractions and the fewer children should be in the same room. The preschool teacher must be able not only to meet the child's physical needs but also his spiritual needs.

Twos are just beginning to socialize. They don't quite know how to share everything at this point. True, they are becoming more independent, but they still require much time and attention. They play *beside* other children and not *with* them. If too many twos are in one room, the teacher spends so much of his or her time guiding appropriate behavior there is not enough time to do what God called him or her for, which is to teach that child about God on his level of understanding.

Threes, fours and fives are learning to play with other children and becoming more independent. Therefore, they are able to learn and play with more children in the room than twos (16 preschoolers as compared to 12 for twos and 9 for babies through ones). When a room reaches more than the maximum enrollment recommended, workers rarely go out and find additional preschoolers. Yes, you *are* doing a great job teaching and ministering to the preschoolers that come to the room. However, the Lord commands us to go into the highways and hedges and compel them to come in. Where will you place them when they do come?

As an example, think of yourself as a teacher of three-year-olds. You have sixteen preschoolers and four teachers in your room. Those four teachers are doing a great job of finding and enrolling prospects, and your room has grown to its present capacity. Now what? Is your ministry going to decline? Are you spending more time guiding appropriate behavior and less time teaching? The solution would be to start another teaching unit. Now let's look at what we have. We might create another room so we have eleven preschoolers and three teachers in each room. Will the ministry and teaching increase again? Chances are it will. There is room to grow and time to teach and minister. Starting new preschool teaching units is mandatory for quality teaching, reaching, ministry and growth.

On the sample Spiral there is a total enrollment of twenty persons (including teachers) in the threes through fives room, which is the correct maximum enrollment. I have placed a plus under the Unit column. When you fill out your Spiral, if you have too many people per room place a minus under this column.

This is probably a good place to say I hope that you will have all pluses when you evaluate your room or division, but don't be discouraged if you are getting some minuses. Those minuses will show you at a quick glance areas of weakness upon which you need to concentrate, and that's a plus!

*Workers*

In the preschool area "workers" means teachers who are enrolled in the room. We do not count division directors or those who may do the records unless they are enrolled in a particular room. When a Spiral is completed on the church level these persons are counted, but when a Spiral is done for a particular room or division, in order for teacher-pupil ratios to be properly evaluated, these persons are not counted unless they are enrolled in a room and teaching. If you are in a preschool room, you *are* teaching whether you are talking or listening.

The chart in this chapter will show you that: Babies through ones need one teacher for every three preschoolers. Twos through fives need one teacher for every four preschoolers. There is an excellent reason for this. Preschool teachers plan, teach, reach, minister, visit, witness to parents of preschoolers and carry out many other areas of ministry. If there are not enough teachers these responsibilities will not be accomplished, or those teachers who are trying to do it alone will soon burn out and quit.

I am a firm believer that when a person accepts the responsibility to teach God's people, whatever age, that person is accepting a very important assignment. A preschool teacher is laying a founda- tion for that preschooler's future conversion. A church needs to work toward seeing that each room has enough teachers so this goal can be accomplished. Each teacher should accept the responsi- bility to pray continually for more teachers and be ever vigilant in seeking the right person.

On the sample Spiral there are four teachers for sixteen pre- schoolers (1 to 4) so there is a plus under the Workers column. As you move up the Spiral and increase your enrollment, you must also increase the number of teachers. Later, I will help you know how to find those teachers you may need now and in the future.

*Workers' Meeting*

On the sample Spiral, three of the four teachers in this room attend workers' meetings on a regular basis. I have also placed a plus under this column. In order for good planning at least three- fourths of your teachers must attend workers' meetings on a regular basis. Three-fourths of 4 is 3, a plus. Evaluate your room and determine whether you get a plus or minus. Now project how many teachers you will need in attendance as you progress quarter by quarter up the Spiral.

*Training Awards*

Training awards are those books we study to help us understand the child, youth or adult we teach. You may also attend a class, seminar or conference about Sunday School work or how more effectively to reach, teach or minister.

In order to put a plus in this column you must have a number of training awards each quarter to equal one-half of the number of workers in your room or division. One teacher may earn all of the training awards this quarter. I am not suggesting this. Try to assist all teachers to go through some kind of training each quarter.

In Florida, public school teachers must have extensive training and schooling before they can obtain a teaching certificate. In order to keep that certificate they must continue their education. They must have six semester hours of classes in their field or 120 hours of inservice training every five years.

As a preschool teacher you are laying the foundations for that child's future conversion, a tremendous responsibility. Yet, we often accept any warm body that comes along, promising them they don't have to do anything but baby-sit. Every teacher should train themselves to do their very best. Encourage other teachers to take advantage of all the training that is available.

As you develop your Spiral, with the added teachers, you must increase the number of training awards.

## Outreach/Ministry

*Space*

The chart in this chapter shows that each person enrolled in a preschool room (preschoolers and teachers) needs a minimum of 20 square feet with a maximum of 35 square feet. Why is the size of the room important? Because the preschool child needs enough space to move freely about the room (he's an active learner). Without having so much room he loses control.

On the sample Spiral, notice that there are twenty people in the room on 10/1. The room ought to be at least 400 square feet, but no larger than 700 square feet.

*Contacts*

The number of contacts made each week in each preschool room or division should equal at least one-half the number of pre-schoolers that are enrolled. And that's a minimum. Check your past attendance records, and you will see that about one-half of the preschoolers attend on a given Sunday. Every absent preschooler should be contacted each week.

But what about those preschoolers who attend all the time? They deserve to know that you love and care for them, and they need a card, letter, phone call or visit too. Many people tell me that their child has never been contacted because they are present most of the time.

On the sample Spiral, I have placed a plus because eight contacts were made (phone call, card, letter or personal visit). Place a plus or minus under the Contacts column on your Spiral. Remember to increase the number of contacts weekly as you increase your enroll-ment. This and the Outreachers column are the only columns that are weekly goals rather than quarterly. It must be done on a weekly basis.

*Outreachers*

Outreachers are teachers who make visits, not phone calls, let-ters or cards. Place a plus in this column if you have at least 1 person making a visit each week from each room. On the sample Spiral there are four teachers. Each teacher can take turns making personal visits, and no person has to visit more than once a month. When you have enough teachers, your ministry improves as well as other aspects of your calling. Imagine what happens to the entire church when at least one person from each Sunday School unit is visiting each week!

## Projections

*Sunday School Attendance*

Place the present average Sunday School attendance this quarter for your room or division in the first block under Sunday School Attendance. On the sample Spiral the average attendance is sixteen. This includes preschoolers and teachers that are enrolled. In order to put a plus in this column the average attendance must be at least one-half the total enrollment. This room would need to have only ten people present to get a plus, but sixteen people are in attendance. I have placed the future projections in parentheses because the present attendance already exceeds one-half the enrollment.

Why do you think the attendance exceeds one-half in this room? Count the number of pluses and the number of minuses under each column:

—This room does not have enough prospects to maintain future growth but otherwise is doing high-quality Sunday School work.
—This room does not exceed maximum enrollment.
—This room has enough teachers.
—The teachers attend workers' meetings to plan for Sunday morning.
—The teachers train themselves.
—The teachers make contacts and visit.

When people (even preschoolers) feel loved and cared for, and they are taught and ministered to by well-prepared, trained teachers, they will attend. Sound simple? It is when teachers take their call by God seriously and do the basics consistently.

*Worship Service Attendance*

Attendance in the worship service (this includes extended session or children's worship, whatever your church calls it) should also be at least one-half of your total enrollment for your room or division. Be sure to count those teachers who attend, as well as the preschoolers. I have shown the worship attendance goals in parentheses on the sample Spiral because the present attendance is higher than one-half.

*Offerings/Baptisms*

Offerings and baptisms may be figured if desired but may not be applicable for preschool rooms or divisions.

Now that you know your strengths and weaknesses (or how to find them) what are you going to do about them? How are you going to change those minuses into pluses? The following pages will help you as you work toward meeting those goals you have or will set.

Preschool teachers: plan for growth, prepare for growth and maintain a growth posture.

## Implementation

### Your Preschool Room or Division's Outreach Ministry

*Enrolling and Finding Preschool Prospects*

At a workers' meeting recently, preschool teachers were discussing their outreach ministry. The director (lead teacher) was expressing his frustration at not reaching out to preschoolers like he should. Mrs. Brown stated that she thought they were doing well. They had twelve to fifteen children who came every week. Mr. Smith pointed out that those children belong to regular church members and that wasn't outreach.

Mrs. Brown replied that she didn't think it made any difference. If people wanted to come to church they knew where it was. Mr. Smith pointed out that preschool teachers had a responsibility to reach out to preschoolers in the church community. He reminded Mrs. Brown that the greatest gift a teacher can give a preschooler is a Christian home. If parents feel preschool teachers genuinely care for them and their preschoolers, relationships can be built and ministry can begin.

Mrs. Brown began to see that preschool teachers must not be content merely to teach those children *in* the room on Sunday but reach *outside* the walls of the church with the love of Jesus.

Now that the need has been established, how do we find

preschoolers and how do we enroll them? On the sample Spiral you may have noticed that room needed to find a lot of prospects right away. One of my favorite (and most effective) ways to find plenty of preschool prospects in a short period of time is "I Know a Preschooler" prospect cards like the one shown.

---

**I KNOW A PRESCHOOLER**

NAME _____

ADDRESS _____

PHONE _____

PARENT'S NAME _____

_____

AGE _____

---

Make an appointment to speak with your pastor. Tell him your concern about the need to find prospects and ask for his help. Ask him to announce your need from the pulpit and have cards distributed in the worship service. Remind the worshipers that they do not have to visit or call the prospects, just let you know the names, addresses and, hopefully, the ages. Distribute the names to preschool teachers according to the ages they teach. Your preschool teachers will have enough current prospects to make that minus a plus under the Prospects column. If you cannot distribute these cards in the worship service, ask your adult classes if they will distribute them in the adult Sunday School classes. You will find almost as many prospects in this manner.

A valuable hint: Follow up by letting the worshipers or adult classes know how many prospects they were able to find for you. Later, come back and inform them about how many you visited, how many prospects visited the church, and how many you were able to enroll. You will gain many supporters for your ministry this way, and they will be willing to help you again when a need arises.

Beginning a Cradle Roll ministry is another excellent avenue for finding preschool prospects. This ministry does *nothing but* look for preschool prospects under two years of age who can be ministered to and hopefully enrolled in Sunday School.

If you want to start a Cradle Roll ministry and are not sure how to do so, the book *The Ministry of the Cradle Roll Department* can be purchased.

Some other suggestions for finding preschool prospects are:

- House-to-house baby hunt
- Salespersons
- Inside church baby hunt
- Parent's Day Out
- Newcomer listings
- Newspaper listings of births
- Parents of preschoolers
- Doctors' offices
- Vacation Bible School
- Bus ministry
- Children on the block where you live

Further suggestions are:

- Use open enrollment (enroll anyone who is willing to be enrolled at any time, anyplace)
- Contact Welcome Wagon for names of newcomers
- Use church newsletter or bulletin to request names and addresses of families with preschoolers who are unreached
- Invite baby-sitters to share names of prospects
- Secure names from day-care centers and kindergartens
- Contact diaper services for names
- Organize outreach projects
- Canvass college housing
- Locate migrants in your area

Now you have a place to start. Having the information is of no value, however, if you do not put it to use. At your next workers' meeting discuss some of these suggestions for finding preschoolers in your church community. What will work? What is not valid in your area?

Write down three or four ways that your teachers will commit themselves to try. Set a date for beginning each project and who will be responsible. You will accomplish your goal if you *plan* to do so. Pray about it, do it and reap the harvest!

Quizzes are fun, if you don't have to be graded on the answers. See how many of the following questions you can answer about finding and enrolling preschool prospects.

### Write T or F for True or False

1. Enrollment of a prospect may be done by mail. _____
2. Preschool teachers should enroll only preschoolers in Sunday School, leaving the parent's enrollment to adult teachers. _____
3. Preschool directors (the lead teachers) should plan for the training of teachers and lead in enrollment efforts. _____
4. Enrollment should never be done by phone. _____
5. The department director (lead teacher) assigns prospects to teachers for enrollment. _____
6. An up-to-date prospect file helps teachers enroll persons in Sunday School. _____
7. When new church members have preschoolers, you may request permission to enroll the preschooler when you welcome the new members into the church. _____
8. Vacation Bible School is an excellent way to find preschool prospects and enroll them in Sunday School. _____
9. A preschooler should attend Sunday School three times in a row before being enrolled. _____
10. The idea of enrolling persons anytime, anywhere as long as they consent is called open enrollment. _____

Did you answer True to numbers 1, 3, 5, 6, 7, 8 and 10, and False to numbers 2, 4 and 9? Remember, an aggressive enrollment emphasis is needed to reach a maximum number of the prospects.

## Your Preschool Room or Department's Organizational Program

*Finding Those Additional Preschool Rooms*

When we looked at Teaching Units on the sample Spiral earlier in this chapter, the importance of maximum enrollment and the reasons for starting new units were discussed. Sometimes getting a new room or place to teach is one of the most frustrating aspects of preschool work.

Most churches understand the importance of finding new rooms for adults when they are needed. Unfortunately, finding places for preschoolers to meet usually does not seem that significant.

One of the fastest-growing churches began to experience a drastic slowdown in growth. The pastor wanted to know why. He researched for the answer. He soon discovered that there were as many as fifty preschoolers in some of the rooms. The preschool teachers had been asking for new rooms for some time, but the church was busy finding additional space for the adults.

Parents (adults) began going to other churches because they didn't want their preschoolers in rooms that noisy (you can imagine) and crowded. Their preschoolers would begin to cry when they drove into the parking lot. Would you continue to go to a church (no matter how well you liked it) if your preschoolers where continually unhappy?

Fortunately, this church had a pastor who wanted to find out why his church had ceased to grow. He started new preschool rooms, and growth began again. He is now, by the way, a strong supporter of preschool work.

Another aspect of finding preschool rooms that is somewhat different from other age groups is that preschoolers must meet in a room or an area that can be sectioned off, producing boundaries. As an example: an adult class could meet in the choir loft; preschoolers could not.

That brings up the basis for the suggestions I have for finding more preschool space. Help your church understand that when there is no more space, the adults, youth, and sometimes the children may need to find creative places to meet, freeing up rooms for preschoolers who, because of their age, are not as adaptable.

Begin by looking for space that is already available in your church. Then, look for space that can be adjusted or adapted. Finally, check out all the space that is within a one-mile radius of your church.

Consider going to two or even three Sunday Schools. Don't

forget, all areas except preschool will double their space by going to multiple Sunday Schools. Preschoolers stay in their rooms (or should) during the worship service. The church will gain some additional space, but not much, in this age group.

*Available Space*

Take a walking tour around your church with the sole purpose of looking for space that is not presently being used. A room used for storage, for instance. Could it be cleaned out and a new Sunday School meet there? What about a large closet? With the door removed and it cleaned out, sometimes even a closet will do. When you start looking with a prayerful heart, you will find more places than you thought possible.

*Adjusted Space*

Adjust the classes to fit the space. If you have a class that has only a few members in a large room and a class that has a lot of members in a small room, switch. Many times those rooms have always been designated for a particular age group. So what? If more people can hear the Word of God, switch them!

*Adapted Space*

One idea that will free up many rooms for preschoolers is round tables for the fellowship hall. That will make for better fellowship for dinners, meetings and socials, as well as make a place for as many adult or youth classes as there are tables. Five-foot round tables will seat adults comfortably. Eight adults or youth make up a good Sunday School class. Using these tables will free up a number of rooms and give those overcrowded classes a place to grow also.

This is not the ideal but it helps when there is a need to reach additional people. You may feel that a room full of adults or youth at round tables would never work because of the noise level. Think about the last time you were in a restaurant. There were people at tables all around you. They were talking and laughing and, for the most part, did not disturb those around them. When you are talking to those at your table (especially at round tables) the conversation stays at your table, as well as creates a sense of fellowship.

Think about the church that began with only four rooms, one for each age group. They began to reach out and grow, and the preschoolers needed more space. The adult class volunteered their room, and they would meet in the parking lot in a recreational vehicle.

Sound like a commitment to grow? Buses, RV's and vans may not be as comfortable as having your own room but, again, if more people can come to your church and hear the Word of God, why not?

*Adjacent Space*

Once again, do a walking tour. Make a note of all the possibilities within a one-mile radius of your church. You would be surprised what you could find. Remember, try to keep your senior adult and preschool rooms at the church.

*Additional Space*

Hopefully, the time will come when you can build additional space. However, as you have just discovered, there are many ways to find additional space until that time comes. With prayer, lots of work and much give and take, there is no limit to how many people your church can reach for the Lord.

## Your Preschool Room or Division's
## Discipleship Ministry

*Finding Preschool Workers*

We discussed the importance of having enough workers (teachers) when we looked at the Workers column on the sample Spiral. Most preschool teachers will tell you they already know the necessity of having more teachers but want to know how to find them. I'm a firm believer that we enlist our problems, but I'm also a firm believer that we don't have to.

I understand that the task of finding teachers is immense. Finding the *right* teachers is an even greater burden. However, the answer to finding all the teachers you need, and the *right* teachers, is not as hard as you might first think.

Sometimes, even when we are doing the Lord's work, we forget that we are not doing this work alone. He is always there, and He promises us that if we ask, we will receive.

Let me give you a six-step method that will help you discover all the teachers you need.

---

### ENLISTMENT OF TEACHERS

1. Pray.
2. Make an appointment.
3. Make all responsibilities clear in advance.
4. Pray again.
5. Make an appointment.
6. Accept a yes or a no.

---

Sound simple? It is. Can this be guaranteed to work? It can because I am not the one guaranteeing it. The Lord is.

1. *Pray.* Yes, you need to do more than pray for the right person, but you do need to start with prayer. Are you doing the Lord's work? Surely He is interested in what you are doing. If you sincerely pray that the Lord will place in our minds the names of the right persons, and you are continually looking for those right persons, a number of potential teachers will be revealed.

2. *Make an appointment.* After the Lord has given you the name, please do not stop that person in the hall and tell them you need someone in the preschool area. Don't tell them that all they have to do is show up. (Enlisting our problems?) Make an appointment with him or her. Tell him that you have been praying for just the right person, and after much prayer you would like to meet with him to discuss the possibility of working with preschoolers. Tell him you observed his love for preschoolers, or that you noticed preschoolers respond in a delightful way to him.

3. *Make all the responsibilities clear in advance.* This may be the hardest for you. Tell him or her that he will have a teacher's guide which will offer helpful suggestions for each week's Bible-related activities. Make him aware that he will be required to attend weekly workers' meetings where he will plan for Sunday morning with the

other teachers in the room. Let him know that preschoolers will be assigned to him to contact, visit and/or minister to. Also let him know he will be taking turns teaching preschoolers during the worship service if that is required at your church. Then, give him a prepared list of his responsibilities he can think about while he is praying about this assignment he is being asked to consider.

You may think you will *never* get any teachers if you tell them all their responsibilities. Yes, you will. *And* you'll land teachers who will do a good job and stay longer. They will know their responsibilities up front!

4. *Pray.* Ask the potential teacher to pray about this important area of ministry and,

5. *Make an appointment.* Tell him you will get back with him for his answer in a week. Make it a specific time. That way he realizes you are sincere, and he knows he must begin to pray about it.

6. *Accept a yes or a no.* After all this he may answer *no.* "But," you may comment, "you guaranteed this would work." It does. A yes or a no is an answer to prayer. You want the *right* teachers for preschoolers. If you have prayed, made an appointment, given all the responsibilities, asked them to pray, made another appointment, and they say *no,* guess what? They are not the right person. An answer to prayer.

You may think this will consume a long time and that you will never recruit all the teachers you need using this method. It does take work. Most worthwhile things do. However, if all your teachers have a prayer mind-set about looking for new teachers, you will have more than one name to consider at a time. Some will say yes. These teachers are those who knew their responsibilities in advance and accepted them.

After you have enlisted these teachers, don't forget that they need to be trained. A well-trained teacher feels more secure about what she is doing and will do a better job.

*Preschool Workers' Meeting*

Remember when you enlisted the teachers you informed them they were expected to attend a weekly workers' meeting? In order to ensure good teaching, teachers must plan.

All people are busy these days. They said they would come to this meeting when they were enlisted. But, is it a waste of their time when they show up? Have your hour of planning time together well planned. Do you have to plan to plan? Yes, but here are some suggestions for you:

---

**PLANNING MEETING SCHEDULE**

Inspiration (5 minutes)
Administration (5 minutes)
Reaching and ministry (10 minutes)
Training (10 minutes)
Planning for Sunday (30 minutes)

---

*Inspiration*

Assign someone to be responsible for a brief Bible study, Bible verse, inspirational poem or story. That person will be there. Rotate that responsibility, and all your teachers will see what happens in a workers' meeting, and that it will be useful to them.

*Administration*

This is the time when you discuss your room's concerns, plan for attending upcoming training events, keeping up with future events in the church, etc. Well-informed teachers feel more a part of the entire church family.

*Reaching and Ministry*

Use this time to assign prospects, talk about ministry concerns, discuss what needs another teacher may have discovered on a home visit, or the joy you received when you were able to enlist a family you had been visiting.

*Training*

This is a short time to have for training, but this is not all the training you will receive (hopefully). This is just a brief discussion or study that will keep you informed on a weekly basis of ideas or methods that will help you.

This is another area where you can rotate the responsibility to your teachers. Now you have at least two teachers attending each week.

*Planning*

The majority of time is allotted to this area because this is when your teachers should plan together for:
—What they are going to do on Sunday.
—Who is going to bring what.
—Who will be responsible to teach in each area of the room.

Planning together, praying together, sharing joys and sorrows, outreach and ministry will draw your preschool teachers together. They will truly become a teaching team that loves and cares for one another, as well as preschoolers and their families.

Planning times should also be fun times. A suggestion: assembling, by yourself, the resource kits that supplement your curriculum can be a job. Plan to utilize the meeting before the kit is used the first time to assemble the kits. Bring scissors, glue, backing (saved from the back of kit and curriculum orders), plastic contact paper, and other supplies needed to a central location. Have some refreshments, music and enjoyable fellowship while preparing the kits for use.

*Training Preschool Workers*

In chapter 7, I stated that we cannot grow churches with untrained workers. That also holds true for preschool teachers. Poor teaching sends more people out the back door of our churches than a good outreach program can bring in the front door.

Preschool teachers *must* be trained to do the important work of helping preschoolers learn about God on their level of understanding. They must know all about the children they teach and how they learn about God. They must know how to teach those children through Bible-related activities, because preschoolers learn through play. Take advantage of training opportunities that are held in your area. Generally, your pastor will be able to tell you what these are and when and where they will be held.

Don't forget those training events that are conducted right in your own church. Encourage your church to begin the *classes for training potential Sunday School workers* mentioned in an earlier chapter. Enlist the whole church in finding potential teachers for you.

*Evaluating Preschool Space*

The chart in this chapter will remind you that the recommended square footage for persons enrolled in a preschool room is a minimum of 20 square feet and a maximum of 35 square feet. The importance of the recommended square footage was also discussed. Try to begin with a room large enough for your maximum recommended enrollment for your age group. For example, if you teach three-year-olds, the maximum enrollment suggested is twenty. Try to begin with a room that will support at least twenty people (20 x 20 = 400 square feet).

## Your Preschool Room or Division's Ministry Program

*Contacting Preschoolers*

Contact preschoolers who do not attend and also those who do. Write notes on special occasions. Send cards on birthdays. Make phone calls periodically, whether the child attends or not. Visit the child at least once a quarter to deliver materials your church may provide for them or just to say hello. Once every three months is not too often to visit the preschooler in his surroundings. Let the preschooler and his family recognize you care.

Make a list of those preschoolers who do not come from Christian homes. Plan to visit those parents, form a relationship, and witness to them when the time is right. Help that child have a Christian home.

*Preschool Outreachers*

Visit to minister, to form relationships with your preschoolers' families, to witness and to get to know your preschoolers better.

There are many reasons to visit. If you are not comfortable going to someone's home to visit, ask someone to go with you. Let an experienced outreacher show you how to visit. As a preschool teacher you have probably formed a good relationship with the preschoolers you teach. Therefore, it is generally easier for you to visit those children you know and love. However, sometimes it is hard for preschool teachers to make a witnessing visit.

Part of the training preschool teachers should participate in is how to make a witnessing visit. That training will make you more comfortable when you do that. Remember, you never go into anyone's home alone. The Lord is always with you and will help you know what to say.

Visit! Visit to witness. Visit to minister. Visit to form relationships—but visit!

### Your Preschool Room or Division's Bible Teaching Program

*Preschool Sunday School Attendance*

When a teacher finds prospects and enrolls them; when a teacher has enough room for those preschoolers and enough teachers to teach them; when a teacher plans for what will take place in that room on Sunday morning; when a teacher trains, makes contacts and reaches out, preschoolers will come.

Doing the basics, just what should be done when someone accepts the responsibility to teach others about God, will indeed work miracles. I've seen it happen many times in other churches, and I have experienced it in my own.

Sunday School attendance depends on the *quantity* of our work (enrolling and prospecting). Sunday School attendance depends on the *quality* of our work (units, workers, training). Sunday School attendance depends on our outreach and ministry (contacts and outreachers).

Then we can project we will have excellent Sunday School attendance. It is like a circle; one depends on the other. It is like a Spiral!

*Preschool Worship Attendance*

The same principles are true for worship attendance that work for Sunday School attendance. When you reach out and minister to others with love and care, they will respond.

*Preschool Offerings and Baptism*

In the preschool area I don't generally fill in the areas for offerings and baptisms on the spiral. Preschoolers are just learning to share. If they bring money they may not give it to you. If they give it to you they may want it back before they leave! However, please fill in this area on your Spiral if you choose to. Most of the teachers in the room give their tithes and offerings through the Sunday School, and this can be placed on the Spiral.

Preschool teachers are laying those important foundations for that child's future conversion. Many who accept Christ as a child, youth or adult can thank their preschool teacher for a pivotal role in that decision. Since preschoolers are not generally baptized until they are older, I don't fill in this block on the Spiral.

Preschool teacher, you are a special person. You are called to an extraordinary ministry, a ministry that goes with that child all of his life. Use the Preschool Sunday School Growth Spiral to help you be the wonderful preschool teacher God called you to be.

# THE GROWTH SPIRAL

Samples for:
Church Sunday School
Adult Departments
Youth Departments
Children's Departments
Preschool Departments

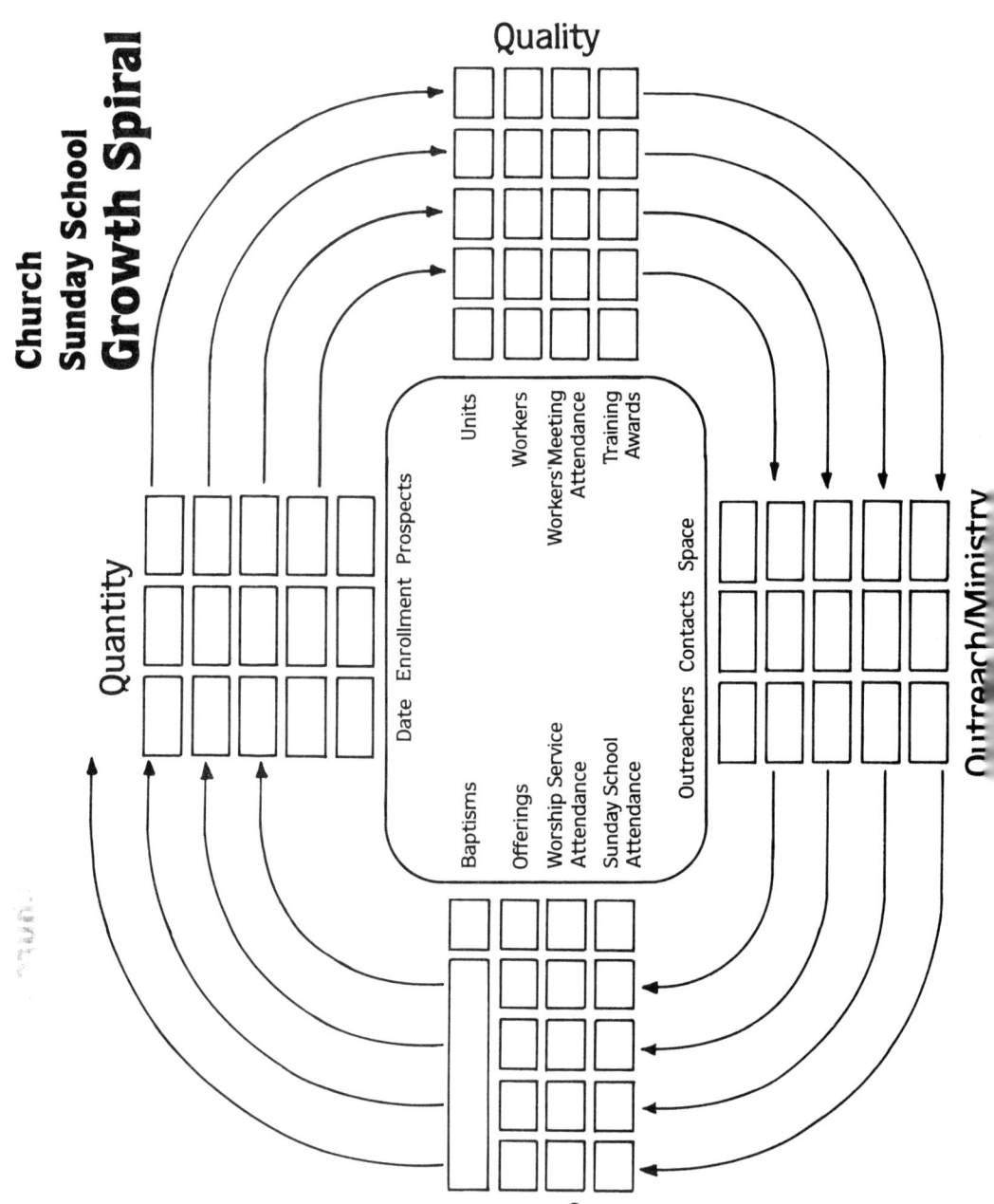

Church
Sunday School
**Growth Spiral**

Quality

Quantity

Outreach/Ministry

Projections

Date  Enrollment  Prospects

Units

Workers

Workers' Meeting Attendance

Training Awards

Baptisms

Offerings

Worship Service Attendance

Sunday School Attendance

Outreachers  Contacts  Space

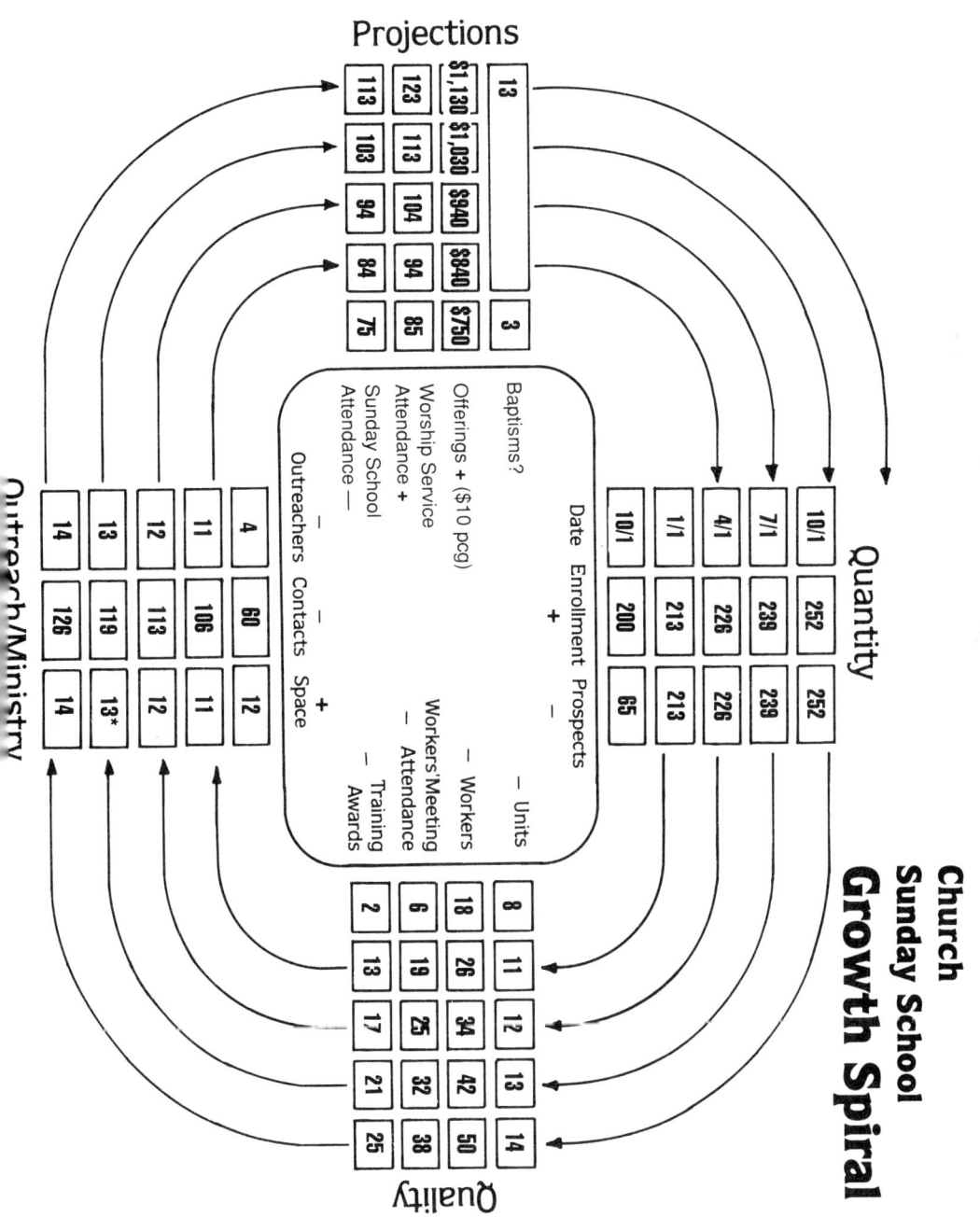

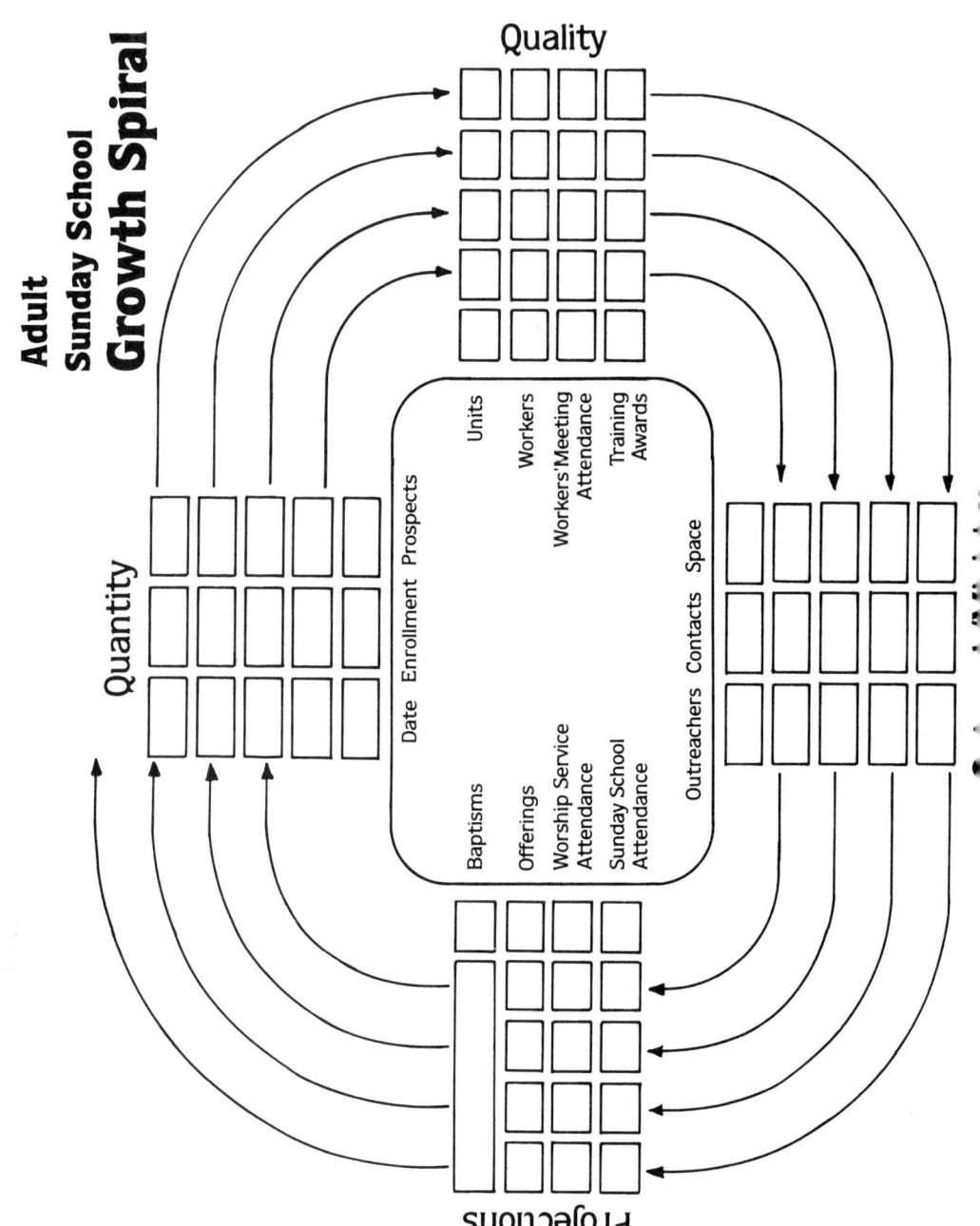

Adult
Sunday School
Growth Spiral

Quality

Quantity

Projections

Date  Enrollment  Prospects

Units

Workers

Workers' Meeting
Attendance

Training

Awards

Baptisms

Offerings

Worship Service
Attendance

Sunday School
Attendance

Outreachers  Contacts  Space

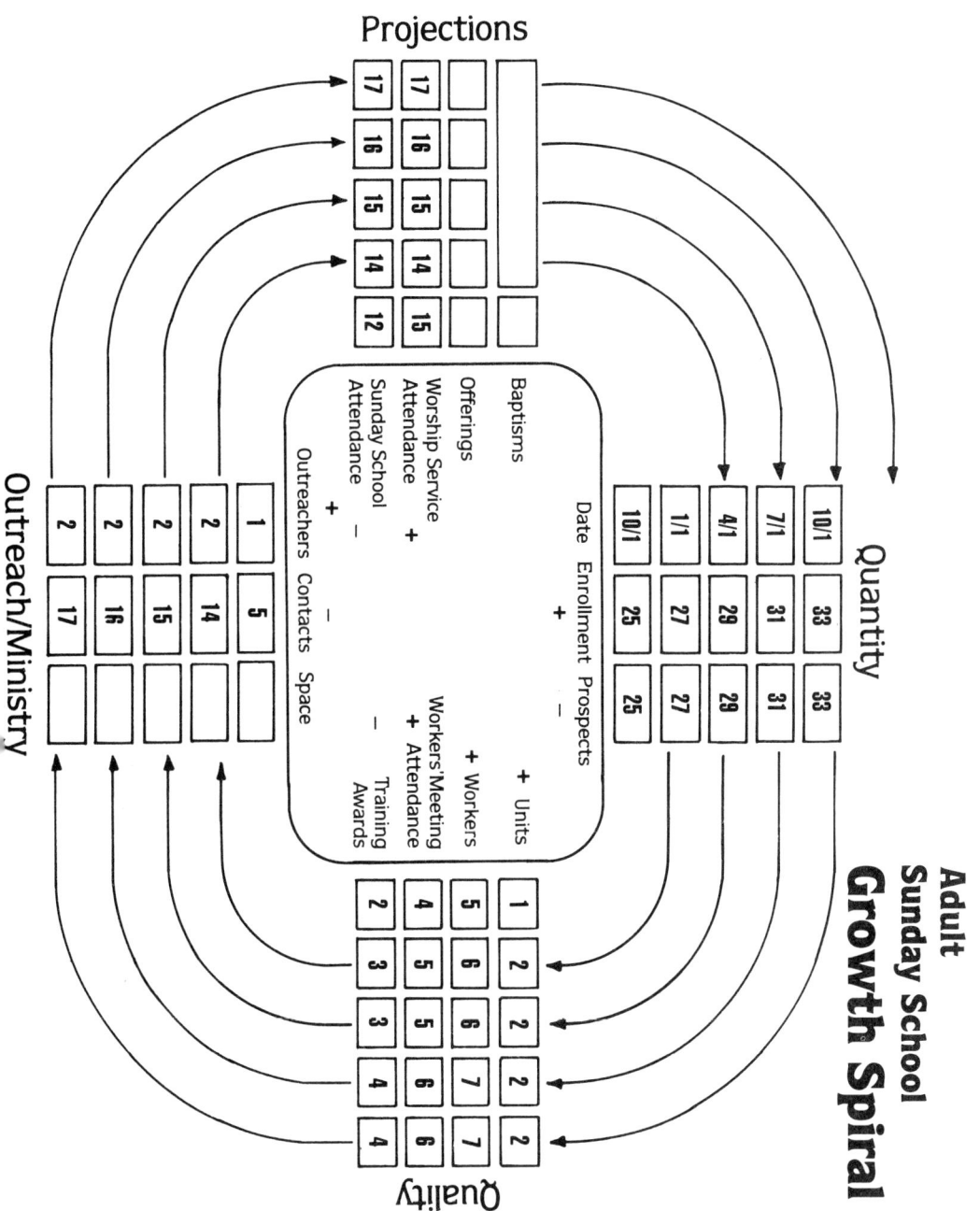

Projections

Outreach/Ministry

Quantity

Adult
Sunday School
**Growth Spiral**

Quality

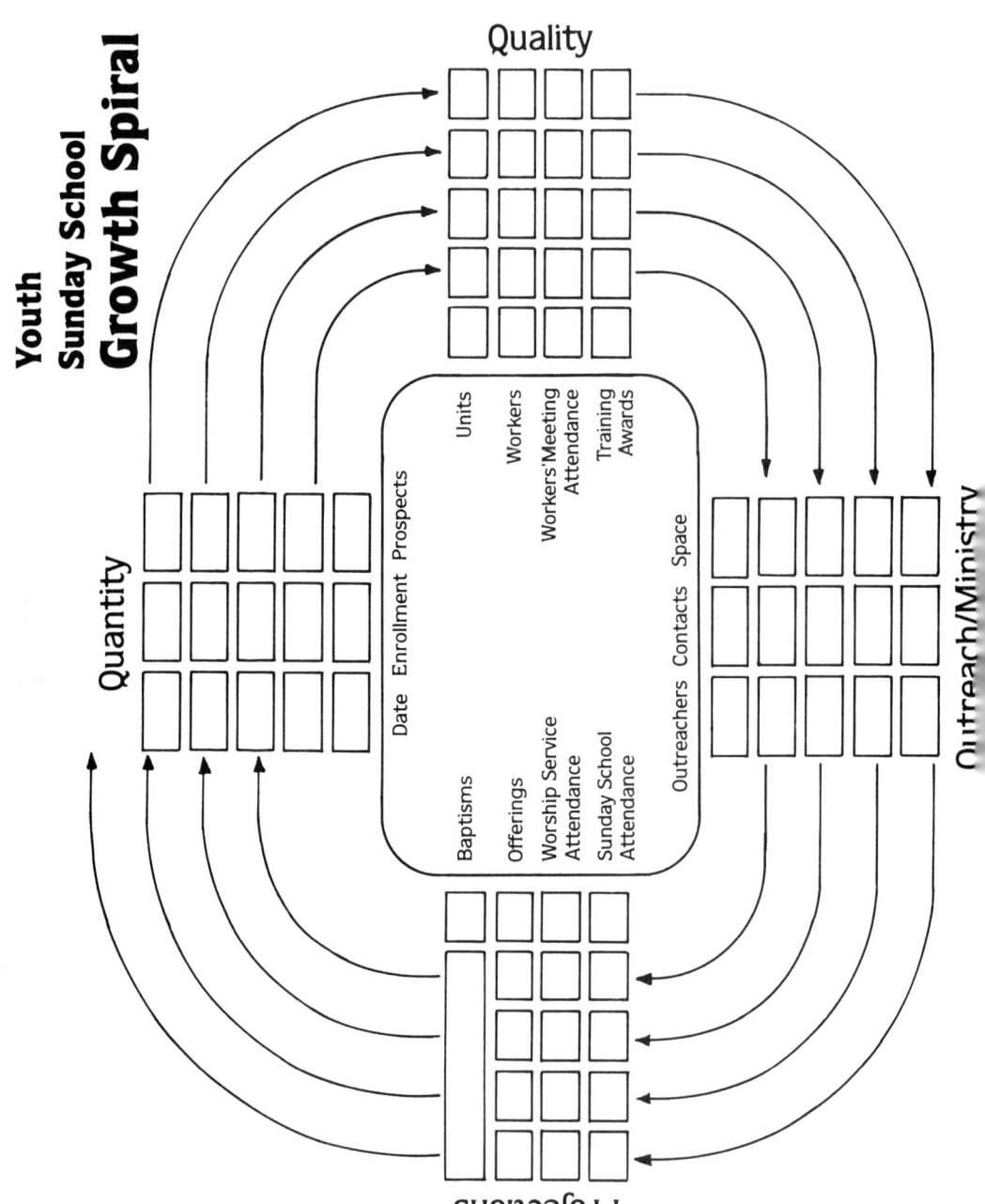

Youth
Sunday School
**Growth Spiral**

Quality

Quantity

Outreach/Ministry

Projections

Date   Enrollment   Prospects

Baptisms

Offerings

Worship Service
Attendance

Sunday School
Attendance

Outreachers   Contacts   Space

Units

Workers

Workers' Meeting
Attendance

Training
Awards

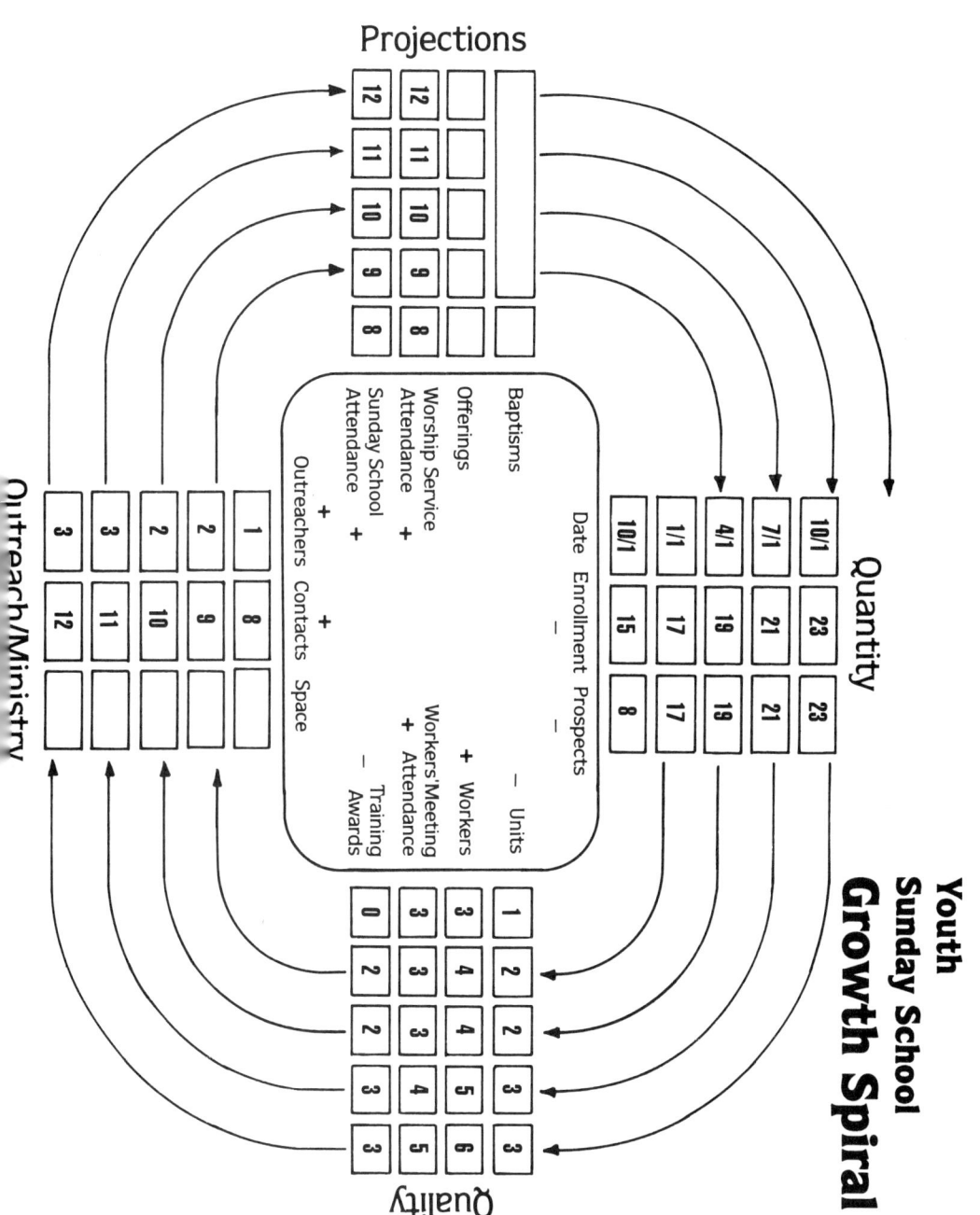

Youth
Sunday School
**Growth Spiral**

Projections

Outreach/Ministry

Quantity

Quality

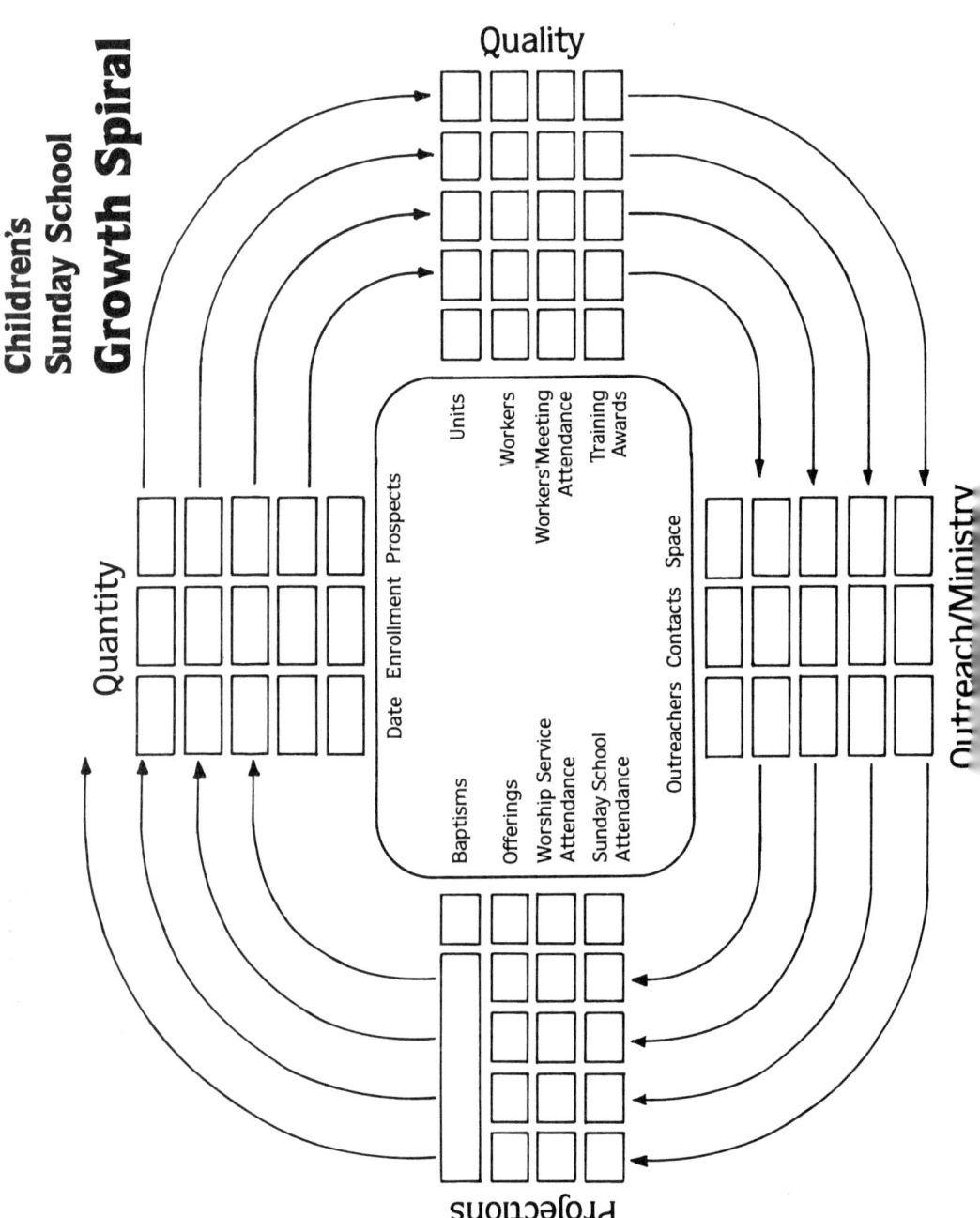

Children's
Sunday School
**Growth Spiral**

Quality

Quantity

Outreach/Ministry

Projections

Date  Enrollment  Prospects  Units  Workers  Workers' Meeting Attendance  Training  Awards

Baptisms  Offerings  Worship Service Attendance  Sunday School Attendance  Outreachers  Contacts  Space

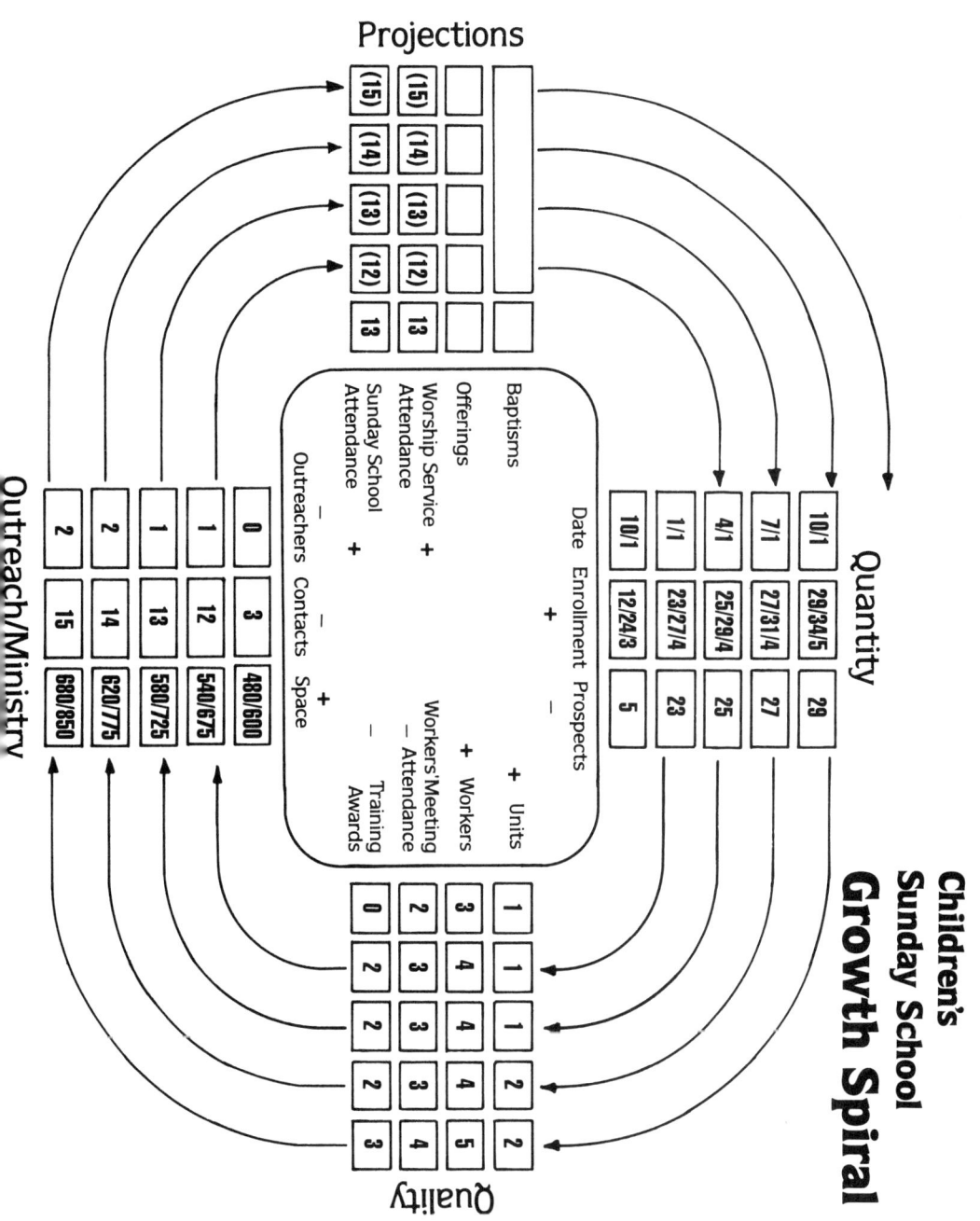

Children's
Sunday School
**Growth Spiral**

Projections

Quantity

Outreach/Ministry

Quality

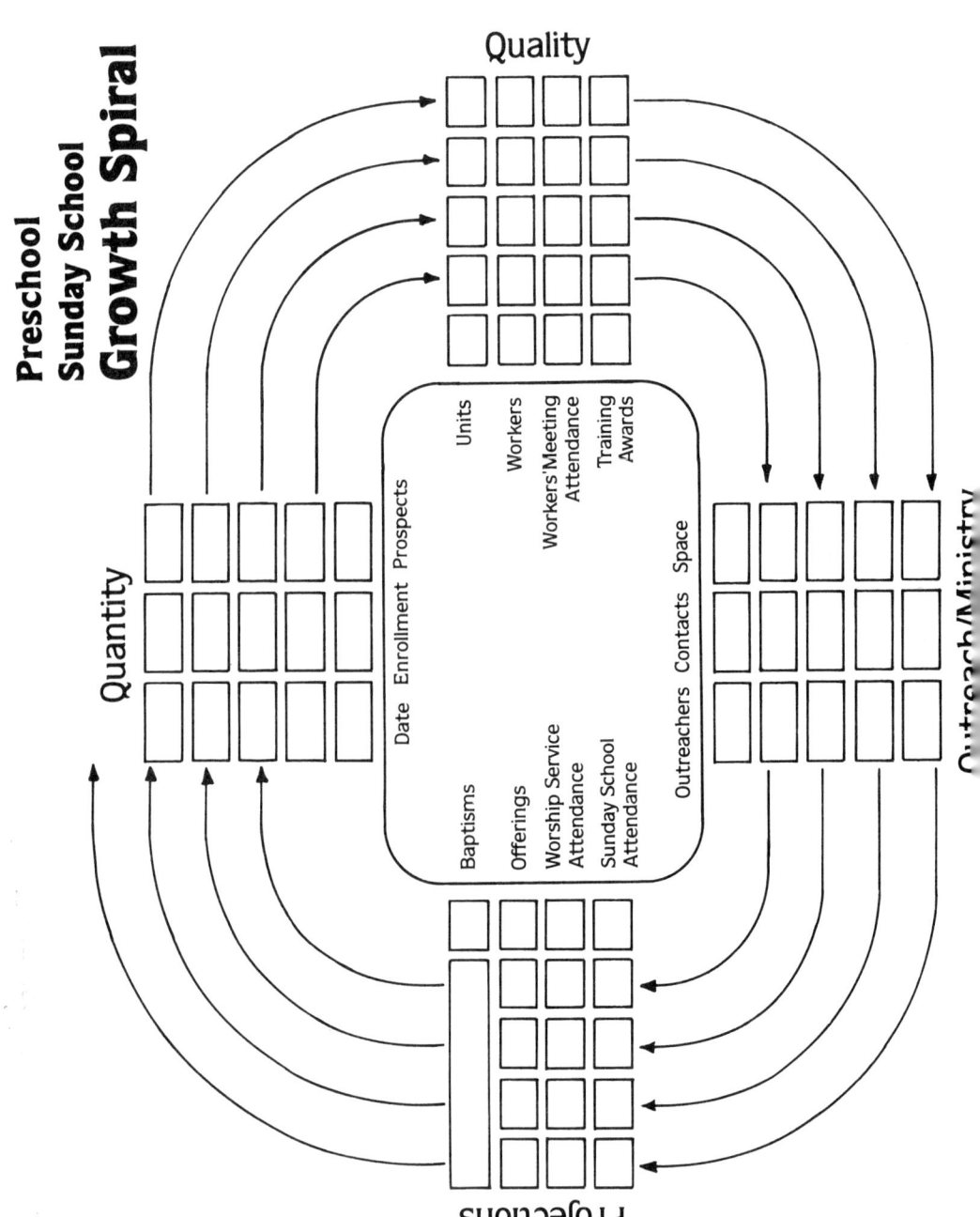

Preschool
Sunday School
Growth Spiral

Quality

Quantity

Outreach/Ministry

Projections

Date  Enrollment  Prospects  Units

Workers

Workers' Meeting
Attendance

Training
Awards

Baptisms

Offerings

Worship Service
Attendance

Sunday School
Attendance

Outreachers  Contacts  Space

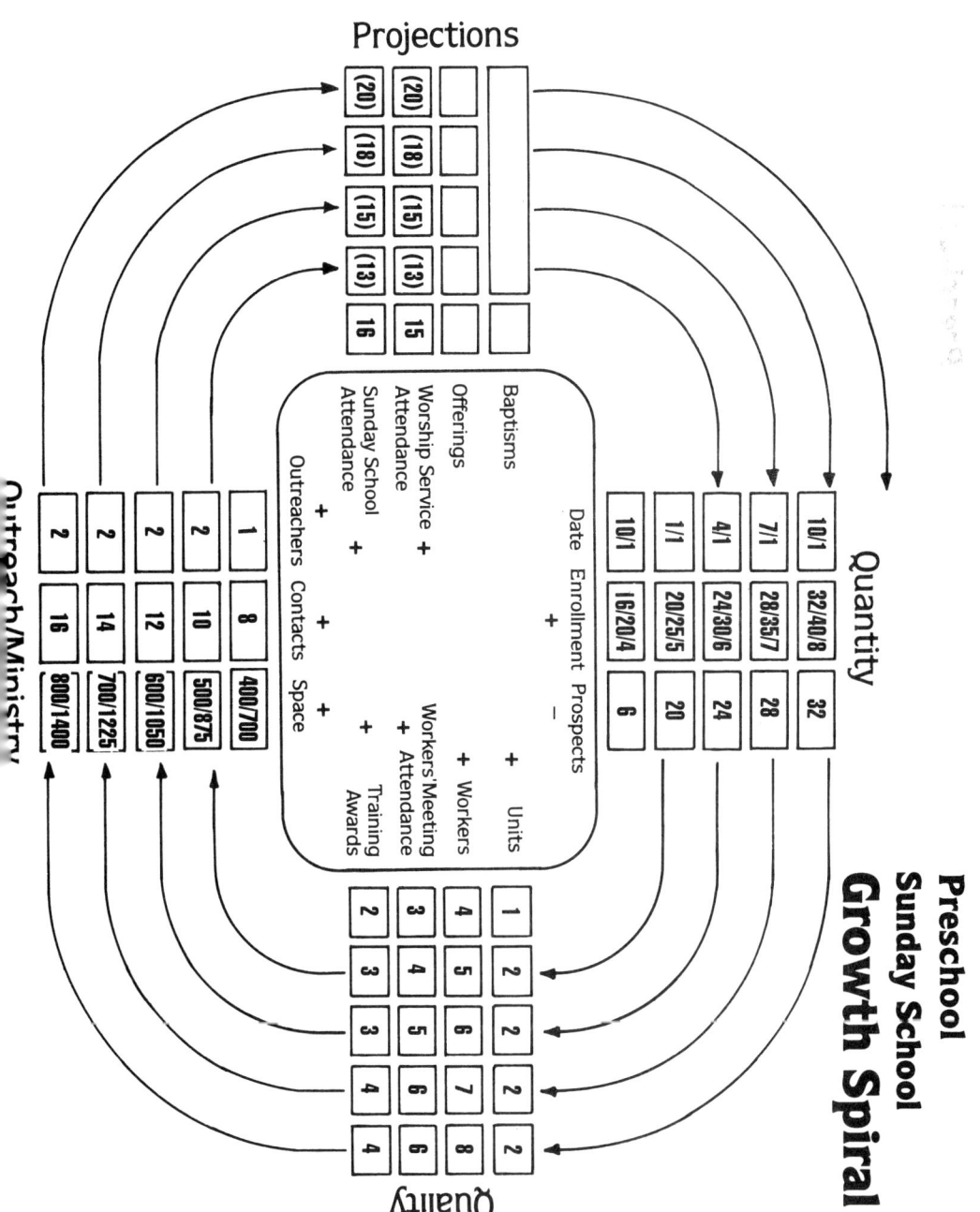

Preschool
Sunday School
**Growth Spiral**